Changing Your Mind
Without Losing Your Faith

Changing Your Mind
Without Losing Your Faith

DAVID M. HOLLEY

CASCADE *Books* · Eugene, Oregon

CHANGING YOUR MIND WITHOUT LOSING YOUR FAITH

Copyright © 2022 David M. Holley. All rights reserved. Except for brief quotations in critical publications or reviews, no part of this book may be reproduced in any manner without prior written permission from the publisher. Write: Permissions, Wipf and Stock Publishers, 199 W. 8th Ave., Suite 3, Eugene, OR 97401.

Cascade Books
An Imprint of Wipf and Stock Publishers
199 W. 8th Ave., Suite 3
Eugene, OR 97401

www.wipfandstock.com

PAPERBACK ISBN: 978-1-6667-1321-3
HARDCOVER ISBN: 978-1-6667-1322-0
EBOOK ISBN: 978-1-6667-1323-7

Cataloguing-in-Publication data:

Names: Holley, David M., author.
Title: Changing your mind without losing your faith / by David M. Holley.
Description: Eugene, OR: Cascade Books, 2022 | Includes bibliographical references and index.
Identifiers: ISBN 978-1-6667-1321-3 (paperback) | ISBN 978-1-6667-1322-0 (hardcover) | ISBN 978-1-6667-1323-7 (ebook)
Subjects: LCSH: Faith. | Change (Psychology)—Religious aspects—Christianity.
Classification: BV4637 H65 2022 (paperback) | BV4637 (ebook)

12/28/21

Scripture quotations are from the New Revised Standard Version Bible, copyright © 1989 National Council of Churches of Christ in the United States of America. Used by permission. All rights reserved worldwide.

To the Pastors of Peace of Christ Church:
Aurelia, Fran, and Matthew

And to My Former Pastors:
Kat, Brett, and Rusty

Contents

Preface | ix
Acknowledgments | xv

PART 1: HOLDING FAST AND LETTING GO

Chapter 1
Two Dangers | 3

Chapter 2
Faith, Evidence, and Certainty | 12

Chapter 3
Keeping Your Faith in Working Order | 21

PART 2: RETHINKING BIBLICAL INTERPRETATION

Chapter 4
Divine Revelation through Human Authors | 31

Chapter 5
Disturbing Portrayals of God | 41

Chapter 6
Misplaced Expectations | 49

Chapter 7
Revision within the Bible | 59

Chapter 8
Ethics and Culture | 67

PART 3: RETHINKING CHRISTIAN TEACHING

Chapter 9
What Does the Death of Jesus Mean? | 81

Chapter 10
Being Saved | 90

Chapter 11
Divine Judgment and Punishment | 98

Chapter 12
Is God in Control of Everything? | 108

Chapter 13
Signs and Wonders | 119

PART 4: SUBSTANTIVE FAITH

Chapter 14
God's New Order: Welcome News for the Excluded | 133

Chapter 15
God's New Order: Enemies and Violence | 143

Chapter 16
The Resurrection | 155

Chapter 17
Learning to Love | 167

Bibliography | 181
Index | 185

Preface

I HAVE THREE AUDIENCES in mind for this book. One consists of members of conservative Christian churches who are not quite satisfied with the message they have been hearing. There are multiple reasons why one might be dissatisfied. But I am particularly focused on difficulties with teachings that are hard to fit with facts educated people accept, or with accounts of the faith that have come to seem morally problematic or spiritually deadening. This kind of dissatisfaction is a matter of degree. For some, it might be limited to thinking that there are questions that have not been well answered. For others, it might arise from a level of doubt that undermines confident belief. However, in a number of people, it is a discomfort serious enough to motivate leaving the church altogether.

My message to people with this kind of dissatisfaction is partly autobiographical. I grew up in Christian groups that I would call fundamentalist. The version of Christianity I learned in these groups is different from the version I now accept. Much of this book will fill in the details about differences between what I was taught and what I have come to believe, as well as some of the thought processes that have led me to modify my beliefs. My discussion of places where I have changed my mind is intended to encourage people who are not aware of alternatives to the version of Christian teaching they now find difficult to accept. Many of them have been warned, as I was, that to question any of the teachings of their Christian group is to reject Christianity. It's this set of beliefs or nothing. My message is that there are often good reasons to change your mind about what you have been taught and that doing so need not mean abandoning Christian faith. In fact, it can lead to a more substantial and more satisfying faith.

The second group I have in mind consists of people who have left the most conservative branches of the church and joined churches that are sometimes called progressive. I actually fall in this category myself. For this second group, however, I have a warning. It is that you can be so pleased with leaving behind what you regard as unacceptable that you do not give enough attention to deciding what you do accept. Some members of this group speak of having deconstructed their faith, but whatever deconstruction is required needs to be supplemented with efforts at constructing something substantial enough to put in its place. Often people who make the move I am describing here are interested in becoming less dogmatic and more tolerant. I think there is merit in both of these goals. On many issues where I was taught it was vital to hold a particular belief, I am happy to acknowledge that it is fine to withhold judgment or to affirm there are multiple ways of thinking about particular issues that should be regarded as legitimate options. But the goal of being more tolerant and less dogmatic does not mean you should simply dispense with having beliefs about religious matters or hold them so tentatively that they cannot guide your life.

Some people confuse tolerance with thinking that all opinions are equally acceptable, which is surely not true. Some imagine that rejecting a narrow dogmatism means no longer having firm beliefs. But firm beliefs are not really a problem if you recognize that you are a fallible human being and that the way you see things cannot be treated as the final truth. In other words, you can believe something firmly, but also with humility. At any rate, my message to this second group is in part that it is as important to discover what you can believe, either as core convictions or more tentative beliefs, as it is to leave behind beliefs that are unacceptable. Much of what I say is directed toward formulating a faith that is worth having.

The third audience I have in mind is people who have given up on Christianity altogether. I suspect a significant number of those who fall in this category have given up because they see no viable alternative to the form of Christianity they have been exposed to. What they have been offered is not something they could accept, and in rejecting it, they left Christianity behind. In some cases, they may have imagined that the only alternative to the unacceptable version that they rejected was a version of Christianity that preserves Christian language, but empties it of any substance. If I thought there were no other alternatives, I would likely agree that leaving the church was the best option.

So, my message to this third group is that you can reject what is unacceptable in narrowly rigid forms of Christianity without abandoning Christian faith and without watering down the faith so much that there is little worth holding on to. In fact, figuring out what should no longer be accepted can sometimes be part of a process of coming to a deeper understanding of the Christian faith. I think it has worked that way in my own case, though I am not claiming the version of faith I have come to is indisputably correct. What I am claiming is that in some cases my revisions are advances over views that now seem to me to be distorted versions of the faith. Even when they are not entirely right, I think they are moves in the right direction. What I say to this third audience may also be of interest to people who have never seriously considered Christianity because they identify it with claims that seem obviously unacceptable. In describing the views I have come to, I hope to give some idea of the kind of faith that deserves serious consideration as a guide to life.

Some people conceive of the options in what I think is an overly simple way. They think of the conservative option as having a robust set of beliefs that does not change, and contrast it with a liberal faith that waters down claims that are difficult. I think this dichotomy is misleading for multiple reasons, but one reason is that there are different ways of being conservative as well as different ways of being liberal. One kind of conservative thinks that because a belief is accepted in a particular group, it must be maintained, which generally leads to a faith that is too rigid to deal with questions or difficulties that might arise. But it is also possible to be a conservative who distinguishes between what is central to the faith and what might be adjustable in the light of relevant evidence. The second kind of conservative might be willing to rethink many things, even while trying to hold on to a central core, and some conservatives of this type might even be willing to consider whether the lines defining that core should be altered.

With regard to liberal Christianity, it seems to me that people typically characterize someone as liberal in relation to particular beliefs. When some set of beliefs is regarded as nonnegotiable, anyone who does not accept them might be regarded as liberal. But since Christians differ over what beliefs are dispensable, what looks liberal from one perspective might not from another. Equally important, the characterization of someone as liberal hides the fact that there are many kinds of reasons for rejecting a belief, and the kind of liberal you are might depend on what kinds of reasons you have. Someone who rejects anything that might be called miraculous is one kind of liberal, but there are also people who reject some claims, which a conservative might think important, because they judge them to involve a misreading of scriptural texts or to presuppose primitive ideas about God's nature or to be morally problematic. The point is that thinking of someone as liberal may not tell you much until you have more information. Furthermore, it can be misleading to call some people either liberal or conservative, since their belief systems may be liberal in some respects, but conservative in other respects.

Rather than worrying about whether an idea is conservative or liberal, I prefer to outline my reasons for accepting or rejecting various claims. My reasons are not likely to persuade everyone. For example, a conservative who thinks all biblical texts are equally authoritative will probably not be persuaded when I reject some biblical characterizations of God as inadequate in the light of the fuller revelation of Jesus. At a different end of the spectrum, people who think that whatever happens must be explainable in scientific terms are not likely to be persuaded by my acceptance of a spiritual reality that underlies and permeates the material order. The point here is that the reasons we find convincing will depend on our starting points. Giving reasons can sometimes be thought of as an invitation to a fuller discussion, but such discussion would often involve something beyond the confines of a particular book. Nevertheless, understanding why I find a particular view persuasive can be a stimulus to further thought, even for those who are not fully persuaded by my reasons.

I have not written this book for scholars. One indication of this choice is that scholarly references have been kept to a minimum. Sometimes I articulate what I take to be a scholarly consensus without providing proof that there is such a consensus. Sometimes I take a position on a disputed matter without entering into the kind of argument or providing the kinds of citations that would be expected in scholarly writing. To do these things differently would have meant a much longer book, and likely one that would be less accessible to my primary audience.

My primary intended audience includes people who may not have much background in theology or biblical studies or philosophy, but who are interested in the issues I explore and disciplined enough to read a book that requires some close attention and thought. A good percentage of people I am writing for won't look at footnotes at all. However, I try to give credit for an idea when credit is due, and I have provided a few references intended for those who want to explore particular topics more fully. References to biblical sources are included in parenthetical notes within the text. Quotations are from the New Revised Standard Version.

The first part of this book (chapters 1–3) addresses the issue of how a mature faith involves both holding on to some beliefs and letting go of others. The second part (chapters 4–8) deals with the need to revise simplistic understandings of the Bible in the light of a more informed view of the nature of biblical revelation. The third part (chapters 9–13) focuses on rethinking problematic teachings that people sometimes receive from their churches and replacing them with more believable accounts. The fourth part (chapters 14–17) discusses some teachings that are of central importance for developing a faith that is distinctively Christian.

My guess is that some people who start this book will stop reading when they find that it contradicts ideas they have not previously questioned, or makes use of ideas that are unfamiliar or create discomfort. Some people may be locked in to assumptions about what the Bible teaches that do not allow them to consider what I say, or more generally to frames of reference that block consideration of alternatives to the way they currently think. But my hope is that for some people, my discussion will be like a breath of fresh air that gives them permission to think about things they find puzzling and consider alternatives they did not know were available. Some may feel liberated by permission to think about matters that are often unquestioned or to find examples of rethinking they can use to make their own faith less rigid or less amorphous. In the end, I intend this book to be an aid for people who are troubled enough to see the need for rethinking some of what is often taken for granted. But I also intend it as a presentation of a form of Christianity that can appeal both to the mind and to the heart.

Acknowledgments

I AM GRATEFUL FOR friends who have taken the time to read and comment on part or all of this book. These include Sam Bruton, Richard Creel, Al Eickelmann, Matthew Hanzelka, and Bob Kruschwitz. Their comments helped me to improve the manuscript, though I should say that I relied on my own judgment about when to follow their suggestions and when to go my own way. Any deficiencies in what I have written are, of course, my responsibility and not theirs.

I also want to think my wife Joyce who read preliminary drafts and made numerous helpful suggestions. She was a source of encouragement in confirming my belief that I had something worthwhile to say and that there were people who needed to read this book. She was willing to do her part in making sure I had time to work on my writing even before it became clear that anything like a book would emerge. Her faith in me was instrumental in bringing this book to completion.

PART 1

Holding Fast and Letting Go

CHAPTER 1

Two Dangers

WE TYPICALLY THINK OF proverbs as sources of guidance about how to live. However, the kind of guidance you can get from a proverb is tricky, since different proverbs appear to give conflicting advice. There's the admonition to "Look before you leap," but we are also told, "He who hesitates is lost." There's a proverb that suggests, "Better safe than sorry," but another one urges, "Nothing ventured, nothing gained." We are instructed, "Don't cross that bridge until you come to it," but we also hear, "Don't put off for tomorrow what you can do today." In many cases you could follow the instruction of one of these proverbs only by doing what another proverb warns against.

Once we notice proverbs can give us conflicting advice, we might conclude they are pretty worthless as sources of guidance. However, such a conclusion is too hasty. While it is simplistic to imagine that having a store of traditional proverbs is enough to tell a person precisely what to do in each situation, proverbs might help in a different way. They might serve as reminders of common mistakes to avoid. Such reminders can be useful, but it takes judgment to decide how relevant or important a reminder is in a particular case. Proverbs cannot take the place of good judgment.

Good judgment often requires you to be alert to more than one kind of danger. For example, you might see what you are doing in terms of not letting others take advantage of you, but if you are attending only to that danger, you may not let your guard down enough to build strong friendships. Or you might pride yourself on disciplined work habits that keep you focused on the task at hand, but fail to notice that your habits sometimes block more creative ways of performing an assignment. In these instances excessive concern with one kind of danger actually increases the risk of an outcome that may be just as undesirable.

FIRMNESS AND FLEXIBILITY

My concern in this book is with two opposite dangers that arise for someone who embarks on a life of Christian faith. One is the danger of losing your faith by ceasing to affirm some essential Christian teaching. The other is the danger of holding so tightly to what you have affirmed that there is no room for welcoming new understandings and rethinking your faith in the light of greater knowledge or fuller experience. Both dangers are real, but it is easy to treat one as all-important while not paying enough attention to the other. You can think that the vital thing is to hold tightly to your beliefs and fail to recognize the need to develop a more mature or a more defensible faith. Or you might think that a willingness to adjust your beliefs in the light of new insights is the paramount concern and change your mind too easily when your faith affirmations are challenged or when they don't fit well with the spirit of the age.

Trying to make sure your beliefs don't change typically results in a faith that can't be examined too closely. To keep your beliefs from changing, you have to guard against ideas that might undermine your ways of thinking. Doing so likely involves refusing to think about views that don't fit well with what you have affirmed or distorting those views into a caricature you don't have to take seriously. What you have to sacrifice is the ability to reflect honestly. You might imagine this kind of approach will keep your faith secure, but a faith with unalterable beliefs is actually very susceptible to collapse. Maintaining your beliefs by closing your eyes to what you don't want to recognize generally produces an internal tension that can be difficult to sustain. It is sometimes with considerable relief that someone who has been trying to hold together a very inflexible faith gives up the project altogether.

On the other hand, the opposite extreme of being too ready to adjust the content of faith tends to result in a faith that is too thin. Sometimes people don't want to give up calling themselves Christians, but they water down Christianity to an extent that it becomes virtually indistinguishable from what non-Christians could accept. They continue using Christian language but empty it of the kind of theological substance that makes a Christian understanding distinctive. Usually some alternative to the Christian message becomes a substitute for what is left behind. For example, Christianity is identified with a particular political agenda, or it is made into a vehicle for affirming the clichés of popular self-help books. When this sort of shift occurs, it is not always noticed. It is possible to lose any genuinely Christian faith without even realizing it has happened.

The ideal is to steer a course between these extremes, striving for a faith that is neither too rigid nor too thin. But what would it mean to recognize both of these dangers? Can you really be tenacious about holding onto your faith affirmations, but also open to changing your mind when you need to? The short answer is, "Of course, you can." However, doing so calls for recognizing when to be tenacious and when to let go of what is blocking you from a more resilient and better-informed faith. Judgment of this kind is often not easy, and there is no foolproof way that I know of to avoid mistakes. You can be tenacious when you should have been more flexible, and you can be receptive to change when you should have stood firm. On the other hand, sometimes you can be fairly confident in the judgment that a particular affirmation needs to be maintained or that a particular faith claim needs to be rethought, and even when it is not entirely obvious which way to go, it is often clear when you should err on the side of being tenacious or err on the side of being open to change.

THE LARGER CHRISTIAN COMMUNITY

It helps to realize that you do not face this task alone. Other reflective Christians have engaged in the same struggle to hold onto their faith, while reflecting on it in ways that sometimes results in altered beliefs. Of course, you should not let others do all your thinking for you. However, it is appropriate to seek out role models who seem to you more advanced. Some paths that you might consider on your own are actually well trodden, and it would be unwise to try to create alone what others have already carefully considered. Discovering how others have tried to think deeply about their faith can also help you to imagine possibilities that were not on your radar at all.

One young man who grew up in a church that emphasized God's judgment and the danger of going to hell was tied up in knots by trying to hold onto what he thought he should believe. He found the picture of a wrathful and vindictive God to be oppressive and hard to square with what he had heard about the love of God. It is likely this young man would have abandoned his faith altogether had he not started reading C. S. Lewis. In *The Great Divorce* Lewis painted a very different picture of hell than the unending torture this young man had been taught to fear. Lewis's fictional account of the afterlife portrayed hell as the result of a choice people make between the only available options: moving closer to God or moving farther away from God.[1] In the story residents of the dreary city, which represents life away from God, can visit the outskirts of heaven and stay if they like. They can choose to be closer to reality, which means being closer to the Love that is the source of all things. Or they can move farther away from reality by building their lives around self-centered desires, a choice that ultimately leads to disintegration, leaving eventually only the remnants of what used to be a person. However, accepting life in God's presence comes with a cost; it involves leaving behind the things that would keep you from participating in a community built on love. If we are unwilling to give up what keeps us from our own fulfillment, God lets us have what we choose. There are only two kinds of people, says Lewis. There are those who in the end say to God, "Thy will be done," and those to whom God in the end says, "Thy will be done."[2] A revised understanding of ideas of hell and judgment enabled this young man to maintain his Christian commitment, even if his beliefs changed in ways that many in his church of origin would have found unacceptable.

I don't mean to suggest that an individual's rethinking can't be misguided. We shouldn't imagine that Christianity means whatever you decide it means or that an idiosyncratic rethinking of Christian ideas can't be seriously flawed. But we should recognize that Christianity is often communicated to us in forms that are deficient. Sometimes we should conclude that the way we have understood the faith is a product of flawed ways of understanding the Bible or of theological ideas that are inconsistent with fundamental Christian claims or of distortions arising from self-serving biases combined with presumptions that people in our social class tend to make. Often, we need to let go of questionable assumptions that are acting as filters to keep us from genuinely hearing the Christian message. Discovering reflective Christians with a wider knowledge of the tradition who have attempted to rethink problematic claims can help us recognize when our thinking ought to be reevaluated, as well as providing guidance about alternative ways of understanding the faith.

Receiving help from reflective Christians in revising what has become troublesome depends on recognizing that the particular teachings you have received from your local congregation amount to only one version of the Christian story. As a university professor, I have found it striking how often students who identify themselves as Christians know very little about the wider Christian community or the historical development of the faith they affirm. They identify Christianity with the teachings of their local church

---

1. Lewis, *Great Divorce*, 69.
2. Lewis, *Great* Divorce, 72.

or denomination and think of the differences they are aware of between Christian groups as places where the other groups need to be enlightened. It is a shift to begin to think of your individual group as part of a larger community of faith and to realize that you can't assume the answers you have learned from this part of the Christian community are the final truth. In the light of an expanded knowledge of Christian thought, it is often possible to appreciate the strengths of the version you are most familiar with, but also to recognize its deficiencies.

It is not just Christians who display ignorance of the wider community of faith. When I encounter students who are militant atheists, I often discover they came from Christian backgrounds that they rebelled against, typically from churches I would call fundamentalist. When these students launch into tirades about the falsehood and the harmfulness of Christian belief, they often display feelings of anger that are fueled by their personal disappointments with churches that represent to them what Christianity is about. However, when they refer to Christianity or to belief in God, they are usually talking about what would be seen by intelligent and reflective Christians with some knowledge of the wider tradition as a particularly narrow version of the faith. These students are often unable to envision forms of Christianity other than the kind they have judged and found wanting.

DOESN'T THE BIBLE SETTLE WHAT CHRISTIANS BELIEVE?

Both kinds of students, those who accepted what they were told and those who rejected it, were assured that the version of Christianity they learned was simply what the Bible teaches. They were not encouraged to think that the teaching they received reflected a particular way of interpreting what the Bible says and that there might be alternative interpretations. It was simply the only way to understand things. No doubt there are some things the Bible teaches that no one who makes a serious effort could misunderstand, but anyone who looks honestly at the range of ideas people attribute to the Bible has reason to recognize that our interpretations of biblical texts are about more than what is on the page. In some cases, we see what we want to see. But mostly we see what we have been prepared to see. We read biblical texts through interpretive lenses we have learned to use that dispose us to notice some things and filter out others. We rely on assumptions that shape our understanding of what we read. We have been taught to make these assumptions and not taught to recognize the extent to which our assumptions may involve disputable claims.

In saying that we need to think of our readings of the Bible as interpretations, I do not mean to suggest we don't sometimes interpret things correctly. However, often we are not in a position to say with any authority that the interpretations we have become familiar with are superior to alternatives. Some of our disagreements are about matters where equally smart and committed Christians come to different conclusions. Often, we need to back away from our confidence that the way we see things is the only legitimate way. We have little difficulty in recognizing that others can be wrong in their understandings of the Bible, but a little humility would suggest that we could be wrong too and that even when we are right, we may be only partially right.

The attempt to understand the Bible correctly has been going on a long time in the Christian tradition, and some of what major Christian thinkers have said on this topic is instructive. For example, Augustine in the fourth century suggests that we can acquire good reasons to revise some of our interpretations of Scripture. We might recognize, for example, that scientific discoveries alter the viability of what we took Scripture to teach. In reading biblical texts about creation he says,

> In matters that are obscure and far beyond our vision, even in such as we may find treated in Holy Scripture, different interpretations are sometimes possible without prejudice to the faith we have received. In such a case, we should not rush in headlong and so firmly take our stand on one side that, if further progress in the search of truth justly undermines this position, we too fall with it. That would be to battle not for the teaching of Holy Scripture but for our own, wishing its teaching to conform to ours, whereas we ought to wish ours to conform to that of Sacred Scripture.[3]

The point here is not that we have no truths to affirm, but rather that we need to be able to distinguish between what is central to our faith and what might be adjusted in the light of greater understanding. Toward some claims, it is wise to take a more provisional stance. Of course, sometimes we do not recognize that a more provisional stance is called for until we try to adjust our affirmations to new discoveries and new insights that come from areas such as science. But Augustine is surely correct in warning that it can be misguided to decide in advance that our understanding of the meaning of biblical texts is unalterable. We need to be open to changing our mind about some things when there is good reason to do so.

---

3. Augustine, *Meaning of Genesis*, 41.

MY FAITH JOURNEY

I hardly know how to begin to describe all of the ways that my own understanding of Christian faith has changed from the ideas I acquired in small Baptist churches in Texas and Southern California. But I'll pick out one strain of teaching that colored everything. Actually, it might be more accurate to describe what I have in mind less as an explicit teaching and more as an assumption that shaped the way Christian faith was explained. The assumption was that biblical stories should almost always be understood as straightforward historical descriptions of what happened. So, for example, the world was created in six days in the order described in the first chapter of Genesis. A talking serpent lured the first humans into disobeying God by eating the fruit of one of the trees in a garden where these people had been placed. God issued commands to the people of Israel to destroy every man, woman, and child in some enemy cities and was angry when the orders were not carried out. God made a bet with Satan about whether a man named Job would remain faithful, leading to massive undeserved suffering by Job.

To question whether any of these accounts should be understood as factual reports of actual events was taken as a sure sign that you didn't believe the Bible, and how could the Bible be wrong? I remember hearing a preacher say that he wasn't smart enough to question the Bible. He told us that since the Bible said Jonah spent three days and three nights in the belly of a great fish, that is what happened. Then, he elaborated: if the Bible had said that Jonah had swallowed the great fish, you should believe that he had done so. Like others, he claimed that if you rejected one thing the Bible says as factually true, everything else in the Bible became questionable. You either accepted the whole package or your faith became a matter of picking and choosing what you wanted to believe.

I now think this either-or choice is much too simple. Is it questioning the Bible to ask whether a particular story should be understood as a historical account or in some other way? Is it rejecting the Bible to recognize that it contains a variety of literary forms and that some of its stories display ancient types of storytelling that are very different from attempts to present a modern documentary? Is it a lack of faith to think that biblical authors are sometimes using poetic discourse or fiction, rather than purely factual discourse?

There are some stories in the Bible almost everyone recognizes as having purposes other than relating historical events. If you think that it is important to believe the prodigal son Jesus described in his famous parable in Luke 15 must have actually existed, then you are misunderstanding what a parable is. It is ironic that the preacher I mentioned earlier placed so much importance on believing that the great fish swallowed Jonah, since there is strong reason to think the story in which this incident occurs is a tale composed by a master storyteller to criticize Israel's tendency to think that God cared only about the Jewish nation. If the story might be like an extended parable, thinking that your faith rests on believing the events described actually happened is a little like insisting there must have been a prodigal son who did the things described in the parable or the Bible is not trustworthy.

I take the Bible seriously, but I understand much of it differently from the way I was taught to understand it in the churches where I first learned my Bible stories. I recognize some scriptural accounts as legendary tales and others as symbolic or poetic ways of communicating theological ideas. I take some passages to convey information about historical events, but I don't assume every detail of an account that refers to particular events has to be an exact rendering of what happened. I recognize that biblical authors presume the scientific ideas of their day and I view it as a misunderstanding to think when they tell their creation stories in terms of these ideas that we should take their scientific views as divinely revealed truth. Similarly, I recognize that biblical writers express their thoughts in terms of the culture of their day, and I don't regard all of their culturally conditioned thoughts and practices as normative for us.

I judge some of what is reported in Scripture to conflict with the overall message of biblical revelation. I read these texts in the light of what I take to be a fuller or more complete revelation that culminates in the life of Jesus. For me interpreting the Bible involves complexities and nothing I heard in the small churches I grew up in prepared me to deal with them. I don't assume I always get it right. I recognize my own reading of biblical texts as fallible, even while thinking I have some understanding of biblical revelation that is solid and secure.

I have changed my mind about a great many things. But I don't regard myself as having rejected Christian faith. In fact, I think of my faith now as stronger and better informed and more mature than the kind of faith I was taught. In the chapters that follow, I will give some accounts about how and why I have changed my mind about particular things and how I understand things now. But the focus of this book is not really on what I accept or what I reject. What I provide is more like a series of examples that show what it means to think about faith affirmations with a willingness to revise them when there is good reason to do so, but also a tenaciousness about holding on to what is vital to a robust faith.

I see the kind of thinking I am illustrating as essential to having a mature faith in an age of competing faiths. In our era there are multiple religious and nonreligious options, including multiple versions of Christian faith. In such a situation a well-informed and mature faith will exhibit awareness of the extent of disagreement, as well as awareness of the precariousness of making faith affirmations.

But having this kind of awareness does not require us to refrain from making truth claims or to give up on having any firm convictions. We can articulate the truth as we see it, even while recognizing that our grasp of the truth is likely to be limited. We can have convictions that we hold firmly, while also recognizing that some of our views should be treated as provisional and subject to change. When our views do change, it doesn't have to be bad news. Changing your mind about some things can lead to deeper understanding and greater insight into the meaning of the Christian message.

Chapter 2

Faith, Evidence, and Certainty

A LIFE OF FAITH is a continuing commitment. But is it a commitment to continue to accept the understanding of Christian teaching that you had when you initially came to faith? In the last chapter I claimed that it is not. You can change your mind about some things without losing your faith. While some components of the Christian message need to be treated as nonnegotiable, there is room for rethinking and revising your understanding of the faith in the light of additional evidence or new insights.[1] But putting the matter in this way raises a question. If you have faith, do you need to be concerned about evidence?

Some people say that having faith makes evidence irrelevant. I have heard Christians say as much, not realizing they are playing into the hands of critics of Christianity. These critics often characterize religious faith as believing without evidence or even as believing against the evidence. Given such a description, they think it is obvious that faith should be rejected. Being concerned about evidence is connected with being concerned about truth. If you treat evidence as irrelevant, then there seems to be no limit to the number of crazy things you might hold to be true.

Some Christians almost invite this sort of attack by talking about faith as if it were an alternative to evidence or to reason. When challenged to explain why they accept Christian teachings, instead of talking about what convinces them that the teachings are true, they say that their beliefs are based on faith. But what would it mean to base a belief on faith? Is faith a

---

1. When I speak of evidence for (or against) some claim, I am talking about reasons to think that the claim is true (or false). Becoming aware of reasons for thinking that a belief you hold is false can signal the need for reconsidering that belief.

reason for thinking that particular beliefs are true? If not, how does it enter into a person's thinking about what is true?

A professor I studied under in graduate school liked to pose the following dilemma for students who appealed to faith when challenged to defend their religious beliefs:

> Either you have good evidence for a truth claim or you do not. If you do have good evidence, you can believe on the basis of the evidence and don't need faith. If you do not have good evidence, faith won't make up for your evidential deficiency. So, faith is either superfluous or useless. In either case it is irrelevant to the question of whether you should believe.

The professor's dissatisfaction with his students' appeals to faith is understandable. Invoking faith is sometimes a way of opting out of serious discussion. If someone asks me why I believe that Jesus rose from the dead, and I say, "I just have faith," I have not really answered the question. If faith is an acceptable answer to this question, then why couldn't someone defend any belief at all by claiming it was a matter of faith? What if someone is challenged about a belief that leprechauns exist and claims that the belief is based on faith? Faith should not be treated as an all-purpose answer to be used when we run out of reasons.

On the other hand, there is something facile about the professor's contention that faith is not relevant to having religious beliefs, since we can just talk about evidence. For some issues, it makes sense to say that the only relevant consideration is what the evidence establishes. We can think this way when we all have approximately the same understanding of what counts as evidence and how to assess it. For example, if we are trying to solve a murder mystery, we have fairly clear ideas about what it means that someone was spotted at the scene of the crime or had gunpowder residue on her hands or was involved in a heated argument with the victim a few hours before the killing. We may still disagree about what conclusions to draw, but we have enough in common to know how to work toward resolving our differences.

However, there are also issues where we don't have the same understanding of what evidence is relevant or how to weigh the evidence we have. We approach things with different frames of reference or different assumptions that shape our understanding of what is evidentially significant. Our differences are especially striking when we deal with matters where one individual discounts entirely considerations that another finds compelling. Something of the sort often happens in disputes about religious matters. For example, a Christian might think that particular experiences of God's presence are important reasons for affirming God's activity in the world, while an atheist might discount such experiences completely. Each might claim to be looking at the evidence, but they don't seem to be looking at the same evidence, or at least they are not looking at it in the same way. So, for some issues it is important to consider not just what we take the evidence to be, but also the perspective from which we are recognizing and evaluating evidence.

Perhaps this is the point where faith becomes relevant. In Christian thought the term "faith" is sometimes used to refer to states of mind and heart that enable us to find the gospel message compelling. Invoking the need for faith can be a way of claiming that to properly appreciate some kinds of evidence we have to be in a receptive condition. Receptivity to the Christian message depends in part on recognizing our need for what Christianity offers. For example, if we resist awareness of the depths of our sin problem, we may be uninterested in the prospect of transformation. Our receptivity is also relevant when it comes to evaluating particular claims. Accepting claims about God's gracious actions to respond to our needs depends on entering imaginatively into the possibility that the claims are true. We might be unable to do so if we are enmeshed in views that make these claims seem impossible or wildly implausible. Some people, for example, are convinced that the only reality is physical stuff and reject the whole idea of God. Some people reject any events that can't be explained in scientific terms. But it is not just our standpoints on factual matters that might block acceptance of the Christian message. We also need the right kind of value responses. If we are not drawn to appreciate what is proclaimed as something that would be a great good if it were true, we are unlikely to be impressed by signs that may point to its truth.

So, we could think of Christian faith as a condition that makes us favorably disposed to respond to the gospel message. However, Christians cannot just assume the condition they call faith guarantees truth. There is room for disagreement about whether states of mind and heart that are conducive to accepting the Christian story actually put a person in a better evidential situation. Nevertheless, if we are reflecting on whether Christianity is true, it is relevant to think about whether we might be approaching its claims from points of view that could block our access to the kinds of truths it proclaims.

What should we say then about the relation between faith and evidence? I think that we should reject the view that faith involves the absence of evidence. However, it does involve the absence of a certain kind of evidence. What we lack in cases where we invoke faith is the kind of evidence that no one could reasonably reject. Instead, we have signs that can point us toward the truth of the Christian message if we are favorably disposed to recognize their meaning. Responding in faith involves trusting the signs

FAITH, EVIDENCE, AND CERTAINTY

that the message is true, even though it is possible to adopt a more skeptical attitude.

FAITH AND THE EYES TO SEE

The idea that there are truths we might miss unless we are in a condition conducive to recognizing them is not unique to religious cases. Consider the role of receptiveness to particular truths in a nonreligious context. In one of Jane Austen's novels a character named Emma frequently becomes convinced of ideas on the flimsiest basis and fails to notice truths that might have been obvious if she hadn't developed such an attachment to her own fantasies. For example, she jumps to the conclusion that two people would be a good romantic match. Because the idea delights her, she does not notice or give weight to any considerations that might conflict with it. As a result, she devotes herself to a comical, but thoroughly misguided, attempt at matchmaking. She misreads not only what is going on with other people, but also what is going on in her own life. In one climactic scene she suddenly realizes that she loves someone whom she had not previously thought of in this way. When she finally attends to the signs of her love, the truth becomes obvious, though she had been blind to this truth before her revelatory moment.[2]

Recognizing the signs that you love someone (or that someone loves you) depends not just on whether the signs are there, but also on your readiness to correctly understand their meaning. For example, you might miss the signs that someone loves you if you think of yourself as unlovable or if you are skeptical about the whole idea of love or if you are filled with emotions that interfere with thinking in these terms or if you are focusing your attention on other things. To feel the force of the relevant evidence, you need to clear away obstacles that might block you from attending to the signs.

One kind of obstacle to recognizing the truth comes from motivations to avoid truths we don't want to acknowledge. Think, for example, about an instance when you failed to recognize some unpleasant truth about yourself, perhaps acknowledging much later what you could not see at the time. Your family or friends may have found it obvious that you were behaving obsessively or vindictively, or that what you claimed to be your priorities did not match your behavior, even though it was not at all apparent to you. We are all strongly motivated to hide from ourselves truths that it would be painful

---

2. Austen, *Emma*, 323.

to acknowledge. As a result, we can resist evidence that in retrospect we recognize as overwhelming.

Often what people are able to accept as true depends on whether particular truths fit into a habitual pattern of thinking. You can have political views or religious views that make it difficult to recognize the strength of relevant points made by those you disagree with. People tend to notice things that seem to confirm their own ways of thinking and to minimize the importance of things that might raise uncomfortable questions. We often adopt a skeptical attitude toward the other side's facts but are ready to accept virtually any report that would support our own position, even when there is ample reason to wonder how reliable the report is. Some of the relevant evidence is not available to us because we have set up filters that block us from receiving it.

In the Gospels there are occasions where people observe more or less the same events but have very different interpretations of what is going on. When Jesus performs acts of deliverance described by the Gospel writer as the casting out of demons, some respond by claiming that he did it by demonic power (Mark 3:22). Where the disciples of Jesus see the work of God, those who find the things Jesus is doing offensive to their own sense of religious propriety construe his acts as a product of tapping into the power of evil spirits. Another Gospel account reports that some people responded to Jesus's signs with unbelief and cites words from Isaiah to the effect that some are blinded in their eyes and hardened in their heart (John 12:40). In one of Luke's resurrection stories two disciples do not even realize that they have been walking with and conversing with the risen Jesus until "their eyes were opened" (Luke 24:31). In another resurrection account we are told that some who were present worshiped him, but "some doubted" (Matt 28:17). Apparently, seeing the risen Christ is not enough unless you have the kind of receptivity that allows you to grasp the meaning of what is happening.

These biblical accounts suggest that the kind of evidence we get for the truth of the Christian message is not going to be convincing to everyone. There is enough evidence if we are prepared to see it, but seeing correctly depends on having our eyes opened. Faith might be thought of as the condition that enables us to open our eyes to the meaning of the signs. Christians have usually thought of faith as a work of God. When you are able to view things with the eyes of faith, it feels less like something you have done on your own and more like a gift you have been given.

UNCERTAINTY AND CONFIDENCE

But does faith bring certainty? The term "faith" suggests divergent ideas in this regard that might seem to be in tension with each other. On the one hand, to speak of faith suggests uncertainty. We sometimes contrast faith with knowing for sure or with having decisive proof. On the other hand, we also speak of faith when we talk about someone's unshakable convictions. Faith affirmations can become so central to a person's outlook that denial of those affirmations becomes virtually unthinkable. How can something be both uncertain and yet treated as a rock-solid certainty? The puzzle here arises in part because we use the word "certainty" in two different ways. Something is *objectively certain* if it is beyond dispute. It is the kind of thing that can't be reasonably doubted. Or since this sort of certainty comes in degrees, saying that something has a high-level of objective certainty means there is little room for doubt about it. However, we also use the terms "certainty" and "uncertainty" in relation to an individual's degree of confidence. When we are certain of something, we are convinced of its truth. We can call this second sort of certainty *subjective certainty*.

Something can be objectively uncertain, even though an individual has little doubt about its truth. For example, suppose you are recently married. When you look at statistics about marital success or failure, you could judge that it is objectively uncertain whether your own marriage will be successful. Nevertheless, even though you can look at the prospects of your marriage from an objective point of view and pronounce them uncertain, you might be very confident that it will succeed. It might even be difficult for you to imagine it failing. In other words, you might have a high degree of subjective certainty (sometimes called *certitude*) about something that is objectively uncertain.

People are often more confident about some truth claims than they ought to be. Sometimes they need to move their subjective sense of how certain something is closer to an objective assessment. They are allowing factors that should not weigh into judgments of truth to have an undue influence on the way they think. However, it is not obvious that limiting yourself to claims that will be accepted by all reasonable people always puts you in a superior evidential position. For example, the perspective from which I consider many questions includes a belief that humans have free will. I am confident of this belief even though I know that there are smart, well informed people who deny the existence of free will. I attribute some disagreements with others to the fact that some people are working from fundamental assumptions about matters such as free will that I think are misguided. While these disagreements keep me from claiming objective certainty, I trust the starting points I am relying on more than alternative starting points that I find unbelievable.

IS UNCERTAINTY A PROBLEM?

Is it a problem for a Christian to acknowledge that some of the central truth claims of Christianity are objectively uncertain? It shouldn't be if we distinguish this sort of uncertainty from ideas that we might associate with it. First, objective uncertainty should not be confused with not being able to make up your mind. To call Christianity objectively uncertain is just to remind ourselves of something we should already know. Its truth claims are not going to convince all reasonable people, but only those who are properly prepared to recognize them. You can admit that Christian claims are uncertain in this sense, but be convinced of them yourself. Acknowledging objective uncertainty does mean recognizing that you could be wrong and that you should exhibit a proper degree of humility about the status of your truth claims. But recognizing that you could be wrong does not have to mean being undecided or being in doubt about what is true.[3]

Second, objective uncertainty should not be confused with acting tentatively or half-heartedly. Suppose that I am convinced of the Christian story, but I recognize that I don't have the kind of evidence that would persuade everyone. If I commit myself to live on the basis of the Christian account, it would not make much sense for me to pursue this commitment in a half-hearted fashion. With some commitments I should be either all in or all out.[4] Suppose that you have trouble making up your mind about whether to go to law school or medical school. You entertain the idea of becoming a physician, but finally decide to become a lawyer. Now that you have made the decision, you shouldn't act as if you are still undecided. In fact, doing so is a good way to sabotage the choice you have made.

One potential source of confusion here arises from not noticing the difference between states of mind that are appropriate for reflection about what is true and the states of mind that are appropriate for acting in accordance with what you have taken to be true. Before you decide whether to start training to run an Olympic race, you might give lengthy consideration to whether you have a chance to win. But to give yourself the best chance of winning when you are actually running the race, you should not adopt the kind of skeptical mindset that might have been useful during your reflection on whether to make the commitment. Living the Christian life will mean

---

3. Newbigin, *Proper Confidence*, 47.
4. Evans, *Philosophy of Religion*, 173–74.

acting in ways that involve taking for granted the truth of Christian claims. This fact does not mean that you can't sometimes reflectively examine what you have accepted as true. It just means that you can't allow a reflective awareness of uncertainty to undermine your ability to rely on the states of mind needed to act in accordance with your commitment.

I have been speaking of cases in which a person of faith is convinced of the truth of the Christian story or, to use a term introduced previously, has a high degree of subjective certainty. However, not all faith is of this kind. Some people can't quite make up their minds about whether Christianity is true. Some might say that such people cannot have faith. However, I think that there are forms of faith that are available even for those who at a reflective level cannot get all the way to belief.[5] One who finds Christian claims credible enough to presume that they are true and commit to acting on the basis of those claims may also be said to have a kind of faith. If you find the Christian story too absurd to take seriously, you can't really commit to living as if it were true. But some people may find the Christian story more compelling than any alternative account that could guide their life. In such a case a commitment to presuming its truth and undertaking the project of learning to perceive the world in the light of that truth can make sense. Furthermore, living in accordance with such a commitment sometimes leads to belief.

REFLECTING ON YOUR FAITH

While reflection shouldn't interfere with living the Christian life, there is still a need for Christians to reflect carefully about the content of their faith. In fact, a refusal to think about what you believe is likely to lead to a significant gap between what you say you believe and what you actually believe. What seems true to people, depends to a large extent what we can fit with our other beliefs and observations. When the fit is not there, we can't just believe because we think we ought to.

People who introduced me to Christianity told me a great many things they said I should believe. Some of what I was taught I still believe, but some of it I have either rejected or significantly revised. Some Christians don't accept the idea that you can be firm about some things but treat other things as revisable. They worry that once you start down the path of deciding that some of what you have believed is false, there is no end to it. However, we need to keep in mind how often the truth we are holding onto may be mixed with error.

5. Swinburne, *Faith and Reason*, 137–58.

There is a place in the gospel story (Matt 16:13–33) where Peter, among all the disciples, comes up with a remarkable insight. He responds to the question of who Jesus is with the affirmation that Jesus is the Messiah (the Hebrew term that translates into Greek as Christ). Jesus gives Peter a commendation for the insight. In fact, he says that it has come to Peter by revelation from the Father. But when Jesus starts to go on to a more advanced lesson about what kind of Messiah he is, Peter will have nothing of it. He doesn't want to consider Jesus's claims that he will be a Messiah who undergoes suffering. In fact, he finds such an idea repulsive.

So, does Peter know the truth or not? The answer has to be that the truth he knows is partial. In one sense he is right in affirming that Jesus is the Messiah, but what he has affirmed is so mixed up with mistaken ideas he has been taught that it is also wrong. What Peter means by "Messiah" is not quite the same as what Jesus means when he says that Peter has spoken the truth. One thing to learn from this story is that our understanding of the Christian message may contain a mixture of truths and falsehoods. We get insights, but they can be combined with confused and half-baked ideas that distort the truths we recognize.

Over the years that I have taught at various universities, I have had the opportunity to observe the educational development of quite a few students. Good students always expect that they will learn new truths. But one product of education that is sometimes unexpected is coming to a greater awareness of the inadequacy of what you think you already understand. When you move from thinking that you understand something to a realization that your understanding is partial and limited, it can be discouraging. However, it is often a necessary step toward seeking a deeper understanding.

You can think that with regard to your faith you have everything pretty much figured out. However, one sign of a mature faith is realizing that what you have figured out amounts to only a limited perspective on the truth. A genuinely mature faith will certainly have places where you take a firm stand, but it should also have places where you recognize that you do not have sufficient understanding to take a firm stand. Such a realization should not keep you from seeking fuller understanding, but that quest is a lifelong project.

CHAPTER 3

Keeping Your Faith in Working Order

IN THE LAST CHAPTER I described faith in relation to the biblical metaphor of having your eyes opened. We might imagine that once your eyes are open, they could never be closed again. However, sometimes we lose confidence in what once seemed clear. Having faith might be compared to trusting another person. If you trust someone, you will generally experience what that person does in the light of your presumption that the person is trustworthy. This presumption leads you to view the other person's actions positively even when a less charitable interpretation might be made. We could say that you perceive that person's actions with the eyes of trust. But you can lose confidence in someone you have trusted, perhaps for good reason and perhaps not. You could get to the point where what you previously viewed with the eyes of trust you now see with more suspicious eyes.

Something similar could happen with Christian faith. You might at one point in your life find the signs of God's presence or God's actions to be clear and obvious, or maybe more realistically, clear and obvious sometimes. But imagine that you reach a point where what once seemed evident becomes increasingly difficult to recognize at all. You might still continue to affirm Christian teachings, but beliefs that are not closely connected to what seems real experientially can turn into empty affirmations that are disconnected from the way you live.

Leo Tolstoy, the famous Russian novelist, tells what he describes as a true story of how an intelligent young man abandoned the Christian faith in which he had been brought up. He kneeled to pray before bedtime one evening, a custom he had acquired as a child. When his older brother observed what he was doing, the brother said, "Are you still doing that?" With a sudden insight the man realized that what he had thought of as his faith was no longer there. He was going through the motions of a religious practice that was disconnected from the rest of his life. When he thought about things in this way, he dropped all pretense of being a Christian.[1]

One striking thing about this story is that it does not conform to a widespread picture about how people lose their faith. We imagine some exposure to facts or arguments that weaken belief. We picture faith as collapsing under the strain. But in this case, it was more a matter of discovering that the faith he thought he had was not there anymore. Maybe it had never really been there. Maybe it had died from disuse. But its collapse was not the result of an intellectual crisis in which he drew the conclusion that some central Christian teaching was untrue. It was more a matter of faith no longer fitting into his life.

I don't want to deny that faith can sometimes be lost because of an intellectual crisis that leads to no longer believing something. However, I think that more often than not, an inability to believe that actually threatens faith is a product of an inability to perceive. If your experience includes awareness of divine guidance and answers to prayer and a sense of Christ's presence as you take communion, you can probably deal with a crisis of belief. In fact, you may be able to adjust your beliefs in ways that not only clear up the difficulties, but result in a stronger faith. But if you lose the ability to have the kind of paradigmatic experiences that nourish faith, then your faith is at risk. Losing this ability, I will suggest later, is often a product of failing to do what is needed to keep your faith in proper working order.

FAITH AS A GUIDE TO LIFE

Should it concern you if your faith is at risk? One way to answer this question is to notice the connection between your faith and your way of life. Having a faith gives you a guide to living that enables you to make judgments of how to understand the situations you face, what to care about, and what to do. In an old, short-lived, television show called *The Greatest American Hero*, the central character accidentally finds a suit that gives him superpowers.[2] By trial and error, he discovers extraordinary things he can do when wearing the suit, but he generally does these things awkwardly through a learning process that is funny to watch. He is not sure why he has the suit. Is there

---

1. Tolstoy, *Confession*, 118.
2. *The Greatest American Hero*, ABC, 1981–1983.

some mission he is supposed to be using it to accomplish? He doesn't know because the suit came to him without the instruction manual that was supposed to accompany it.

I assume that you don't have a suit that gives you superpowers, but in some ways, you face a similar problem. Life would be easier to navigate if you had something like an instruction manual that told you what it was about and how to live it. For people with religious faith, Scriptures perform this kind of function. Think, for example, about the Jewish tradition. The central idea for Jews is that God has by various redemptive acts brought the Jewish people into existence and graciously laid out for them a way of life that is described in Hebrew Scriptures. This way of life includes specific commands, which are often referred to as the Law. But that translation of the Hebrew term "*Torah*" seems inadequate when we try to understand Jewish attitudes toward these commands. If you think of law as just a list of restrictions, it will be hard to see how someone could get very excited about receiving it. Who wants to be told what to do? But in the Psalms Jewish writers talk about God's law as a wonderful thing that they treasure and meditate on day and night. Why so?

The answer seems to be that they think of God's law as something like a set of instructions that provide guidance about how to live, and they are grateful for the help. Imagine that you were lost in the woods and didn't have a clue about how to find your way. Then imagine that you discover a map that enables you to determine your location and to reach a path that will help you discover what direction to go. That situation is something like what the Psalmist must have in mind when proclaiming that God's law is a "lamp to my feet and a light to my path" (Ps 119:105). It provides directions to fruitful and productive living that come from a caring and wise source. Heeding this instruction can save a person from needless floundering.

Christian faith can be thought of in a similar way. It is a grateful response to God's redemptive acts that have made possible a new identity and a new mode of life. Accepting this new way of life ordinarily means seeing the futility of other ways of living and feeling the attraction of a life that is attuned to what God intends us to be. Included in this response is a commitment to follow teachings that lay out for us a program for putting away our destructive tendencies and becoming involved in God's redemptive work. In taking up the task of discipleship to Christ, we discover what we need to care about and what we need to be doing. To have this sort of faith is to have a vision of what life is about that guides and sustains us.

By contrast losing your faith means losing the kind of orientation that allowed you to discover this new identity and shape your way of life. Conceivably someone could lose any sense of what life is about and how to live it. But in practice losing your faith usually means something else. Since you need some kind of guide to find your way around in life, losing confidence in the message of one faith typically means acquiring a different faith. That other faith might be a religious alternative, or it might be a nonreligious one. For example, someone who loses confidence in a Christian understanding of things might turn to a secular faith that declares the ultimate reality is physical stuff and humans are an unintended byproduct of the physical system. Connected with this view of things, of course, are very different accounts of how to live.[3]

PROTECTING YOUR FAITH

When you find something valuable, you generally want to protect it. Some things we try to protect by putting them away and not using them. Perhaps we take out fragile items occasionally to admire, but we don't subject them to the dangers of careless treatment that might break them. They are items we unwrap and display for special occasions, but are definitely not for everyday use.

Some people try to treat their faith in a similar way. They want to keep it secure and make sure it isn't damaged. They try to preserve it in the pristine condition it was in when they received it. In effect they put it in a box that they reserve for sacred things. It turns out, however, that this strategy of protection does not work well with faith. One reason is that faith either develops or stagnates, depending on how we use it. Trying to keep it secure by putting it away is a little like trying to preserve a musical talent by not singing or playing an instrument. If you put your faith away to keep it secure, it is not likely to be there when you try to pull it out of storage.

Another reason that you can't protect faith by putting it in a box is that doing so means separating it from the rest of what you think about. However, you don't really understand religious concepts or religious doctrines if you can't connect them to the thinking about things that you have acquired from nonreligious contexts. For example, if someone says that God is good, you have to be able to relate what is said to what you already know about goodness. If the teaching is about salvation, you have to use terms from human experience to make sense of the concept. If you are taught about creation, you will need to relate this teaching to the understanding of the natural order you have acquired from science. The task of understanding

---

3. For a fuller account of the need for orienting stories as a guide to life, see my book, *Meaning and Mystery*.

calls for a willingness to explore religious ideas by asking questions about what you find puzzling.

When I was nine or ten, I remember asking a Sunday School teacher about some religious teaching that puzzled me. I can recall clearly the teacher's answer to my question. He said, "Well, you just have to have faith." I am sure that this answer seemed like a perfectly good reply to the teacher, but it left me unsatisfied. Even at this young age, I drew the conclusion that the teacher didn't know how to answer the question that troubled me. It also seemed to me that the response he gave communicated something else: I shouldn't be asking this kind of question. Implicitly I was being told people who have enough faith don't need such answers. With things that seem unbelievable or puzzling, we should simply accept what we have been taught. I admit there is sometimes wisdom in accepting what you have been taught. What we are unprepared to understand at one point in our development may become clearer later. But if you think you shouldn't even try to understand something that makes little sense to you, you can end up repeating empty words that can't carry much conviction.

In retrospect it seems to me that I was being taught to fear that if I asked too many questions, I would get to the point where the lack of answers would mean losing my faith. So, it was better to stop before I got myself into trouble. The problem with that lesson, however, is that a faith you are afraid might collapse when questioned is difficult to sustain. If you are worried that you might lose your faith if you think hard, you need to stay away from anything that might cause you to think hard. That means not reading the wrong books or getting into conversations with the wrong people. It also means hiding from yourself the questions or doubts you are afraid will become big enough to topple that fragile faith.

It might come as a surprise, but to protect your faith, you need to allow it to get bruised a little. You need to deal directly with the things that puzzle you. What you sweep under the rug tends to show up again in some form. In my own case, once I learned to face up to challenges to my faith, I became more confident that it wasn't in as much danger of collapse as I had imagined. But to face these challenges, I couldn't cling to the illusion of infallibility. I had to recognize that my own understanding at any given time was partial and subject to error. I could get a faith that was stronger and better able to withstand challenges that might arise only by changing my mind about ideas that couldn't withstand the challenges. I think when I became less afraid of losing my faith, I was better prepared to develop the kind of faith I could protect.

LIVING A LIFE OF FAITH

While we can think of faith as a gift, we need to remember that it is the kind of gift that calls for continuing effort on our part. Compare it to the gift of a college education. Imagine some benefactor has paid for your education. Such a gift is not like a television set that you can just take out of the box and plug in. It is instead an opportunity whose value won't be realized unless you invest yourself in a process that results in real learning. If you don't go to class and don't read your assignments, you give some indication that you don't really understand or don't appreciate the value of what you have received. But if you apply yourself diligently, the result may be the kind of benefit the giver hoped to bestow.

The point of the gift of faith is to enable you to live a life of faith. If you have accepted the Christian message as true, you have made a first step. But having a faith you can live by means learning to perceive the events of your life in the light of the Christian story. In other words, it is not enough to affirm particular teachings as true; you need to integrate these truths into the way you think and the way you feel so that you come increasingly to experience things in ways that fit with what you have affirmed.

To see what I mean, imagine accepting a teaching about how to live that differs from the Christian message. The Stoic philosopher Epictetus believed that the secret of good living was to distinguish between what is in your control and what is not in your control.[4] He thought that if we could learn not to react to things outside of our control as if they were in our control, we could avoid the disappointment and frustration that we needlessly bring on ourselves. Epictetus taught that our control is limited to things internal to our minds, i.e., our thoughts, desires, and emotional reactions. Anything external to the mind, he said, we should regard as beyond our control. He realized it wasn't enough for someone to agree that his teaching is true. He proposes a series of practices designed to help his followers over time bring their experience into line with these teachings.

For example, he suggests naming things in ways that makes it evident when events are beyond our control. If you break a vase, learn to think it was a vase you broke, which reminds you that vases are the kind of things that break. Another piece of instruction offered by Epictetus is to learn to think about tragedies that happen to us as we would if it had happened to someone we didn't know. If you can develop the habit of habitually viewing events in your own life from this more objective perspective, you can see what happens as expressions of a larger order that is beyond your control.

---

4. Epictetus, *Enchiridion*, 17.

Doing so should make you less vulnerable to disturbing emotions that don't fit with the teaching you have affirmed.

While I think there is real insight in Epictetus, I don't fully accept his vision of how to live. Nevertheless, this example illustrates how what we affirm intellectually does not automatically become real to us. Sometimes it takes a process to bring the way we experience our world closer to what we have accepted as true. You may affirm that Christ has defeated the powers of sin and death, but it often won't feel that way. You may affirm that God is working in the world to achieve redemptive purposes, but often those purposes seem hidden from view. Like the followers of Epictetus, we need to acquire the kinds of thoughts, attitudes, and emotions that will enable us to perceive the events of our lives in a way that is shaped by the Christian message. In other words, we need to submit ourselves to a process that develops our faith.

We build our faith primarily by devoting ourselves to spiritual disciplines that nourish it. It is through participation in activities such as communal worship, prayer, the study of Scripture, and deliberate acts of service that we enhance our ability to internalize the kind of perspective that enables us to see what might otherwise be hidden from view. I recall many years ago when someone who was not a Christian asked me why I went to church. The answer I gave was that I went to remind myself of what I believed. While such an answer is not a full explanation, it does highlight something significant. Intentionally remembering things that we hold to be important helps to make them important in our lives. Rituals that involve dramatic enactments of our beliefs help us to bring what we affirm closer to our experience.

KINGDOM VALUES

Perceiving correctly is not just a matter of getting the facts right. It is also a matter of recognizing and identifying with values that are explicitly or implicitly contained within the Christian message. Jesus taught that the values of the kingdom are different from the values our world socializes us into. For example, becoming his disciple means coming to recognize that it is not earthly power or glory that we should aspire to, but humble service. Some of the values of the kingdom of God might seem ridiculous to us because they are so out of sync with values we have been conditioned to accept. Building our faith involves learning to replace some of our conditioned responses with values rooted in a Christian understanding.

It is easy to get caught up in cultural systems you come to take for granted. I am not just talking about things that everyone recognizes as bad, but rather things that might be good in some ways, but potentially compete with devotion to Christ. It is good to pursue a career, but you can internalize ideas of success that are antithetical to the Christian message. It is good to love your country, but you can easily come to justify things done in the name of patriotism that conflict with the central thrust of Christian teaching. Keeping your faith in working order calls for being alert to the ways that sources alien to the Christian message may be shaping your values.

Some of what we need to be alert to comes from well-meaning preachers or teachers who bring us distorted versions of Christianity. In some cases, they are merely passing on what they have heard. But many popular versions of the Christian message seem almost calculated to tell us what we want to hear while shielding us from what conflicts with our prejudices and our self-serving biases. Sometimes Christianity is portrayed as a kind of how-to guide for achieving individual prosperity. Sometimes it is presented as a message about preparing for life after death that relieves us of responsibility for improving things in this world. Often Christian teaching is used to support ideas that make us feel superior to other people and judgmental towards them. The Christian message is even combined with militaristic values that clearly conflict with Jesus's teachings. It can be disconcerting to try to lay aside ideas we find comforting or familiar in order to genuinely hear the biblical message. But often that is precisely what we need to do to keep our faith in working order.

PART 2

Rethinking Biblical Interpretation

CHAPTER 4

Divine Revelation through Human Authors

ONE WAY TO LOSE your faith is to study the Bible. I don't mean studying it in a typical church Bible study group. I mean studying it in an academic setting where you encounter serious critical analysis of biblical texts in their historical and cultural contexts. You learn to read the Bible as you might read other ancient texts and to ask the kinds of questions that don't come up in most church settings. The results can be unsettling. You discover how closely some biblical texts resemble writings from other ancient Near Eastern nations that you recognize as examples of ancient myth or legend. You notice how biblical stories with historical content show signs of being shaped by recognizable ideological or political agendas. You find conflicting accounts of the same events, as well as conflicting theological views by different biblical authors. In short, the Bible starts to look to you like a more human book than you expected.

While some conclusions drawn by biblical scholars arise from skeptical assumptions that can be rejected, many of their claims turn out to be based on convincing evidence that is hard to deny without closing your eyes to the facts. But recognizing the validity of the well-attested results of biblical scholarship doesn't fit easily with the way many Christians have learned to think about the Bible. Christians who become informed about such scholarship often find that holding onto their faith requires them to let go of assumptions about the nature of biblical revelation they acquired in church.

Most of my earliest ideas about the Bible came through Sunday school classes. These classes gave me a wealth of Bible stories. Along with the stories, there were verses to memorize and doctrinal instruction about what the Bible teaches. We didn't have a written catechism, but we did learn to recite standard answers to questions about what we should believe. In addition to these classes, I tried to read the Bible on my own as soon as I was able to read much at all. When I was probably around 9 or 10, I decided to try to read the Bible all the way through, starting at the beginning. Someone had told me that if I read three chapters each day and five on Sunday, I could finish the whole Bible in a year's time. It would be an understatement to say that I was unprepared for this venture. I am not sure how far I made it, but I tried, not even skipping the genealogies or instructions on how to construct the Tabernacle, do sacrifices, and observe the food laws. No doubt my "reading" often consisted of going over words on the page while my mind wandered, as I legalistically plowed ahead. But even if I had been a more diligent and a more mature reader, the ways I had been taught to think about the Bible would have hindered me from moving beyond a Sunday-school level of understanding.

Early on I had been told that the Bible came from God. It was regularly referred to as the word of God. While no one ever explained exactly what that meant, I got the impression that the words in the biblical text were just what God wanted to be there. I remember hearing warnings from the pulpit quoting from the book of Revelation, but applied to the Bible as a whole, against making any alterations to the biblical text. Along with the idea that the words of the Bible came from God was the teaching that what the Bible said was completely true. It was possible, of course, to misunderstand the Bible, but when properly understood, I was assured that it was absolutely reliable. If God was perfect and all-knowing, it seemed reasonable to expect that God's message to the world must be perfect as well.

This kind of reasoning about what the Bible must be like turns out to be in tension with actually paying close attention to biblical texts and asking adult questions about them. Even as a child, I remember being puzzled by things in the Bible that did not seem to fit with the claim that what the Bible said was a message directly from God, but it was only after I had taken college courses on the Bible and read serious books about it that I realized I needed to significantly revise how I thought about these matters.

What I learned about the Bible in college courses and through my own reading was to a large extent a recapitulation of what educated Christians had been learning about it since the nineteenth century when historical-critical ways of studying the Bible were systematically applied. But in retrospect what seems striking to me is how little my church training had prepared me to deal with a range of facts that were well known to Christians who had done this kind of study. I now recognize that even teachers from colleges and seminaries who occasionally spoke at our church tended to ignore or dismiss uncomfortable findings of biblical scholarship. Some of these teachers may have been the product of an education that taught them to reject such things. Others were likely better informed, but reluctant to rock the boat by bringing up matters that would challenge our preconceptions. Nevertheless, it eventually became evident to me that thinking about the Bible in a way that did justice to the facts meant giving up the simplistic pictures I had acquired in church about what it means to view the Bible as coming from God.

HUMAN AUTHORS AND THEIR AUDIENCES

When people told me that the Bible came from God, they didn't mean to deny that it had human authors. However, in our reading of biblical texts the role of these human authors tended to be minimized, since the writers of biblical texts were assumed to be getting the scoop directly from God. Perhaps God didn't dictate the exact words, but God was thought to be pulling the strings behind the scenes to make sure that the human authors said just what needed to be said and didn't make any mistakes.

There are many ways to think about the significance of human authorship of Scripture, but I want to concentrate in this chapter on an aspect of authorship that strikes me as very important for thinking about how the Bible can be viewed as a revelation of God. It is the fact that each human author lives at a particular time and place and writes for an audience of the same period in a way that is comprehensible to that audience. By itself, such a fact seems obvious, but its implications are far-reaching. Biblical authors speak a particular language and have a particular understanding of what the world is like. They are members of a particular culture and share assumptions made by people in that culture. What they write is directed to people who share their way of thinking.

A little reflection should make it evident that people of our time are not members of the audiences for which biblical authors were writing. We come from different cultures and have beliefs and ways of thinking that have been shaped by developments that these authors could not have anticipated. The point is not that you can't learn from a biblical author. It is instead that reading someone who makes assumptions that you do not accept adds a level of complexity. You have to enter into the biblical author's thought world enough to comprehend what a text would have meant to its original recipients, but you also need to ask how such a message can make sense to someone who lives in a different thought world.

Here is one example: When biblical writers talk about creation, they do not speak from the perspective of someone with a twenty-first century understanding of science. Instead they assume the standard view of the nature of the world accepted at their time. Hence, in the story in the first chapter of Genesis, one of the created things is what some older English translations call a firmament. The firmament is some sort of barrier dividing waters above the sky from the land inhabited by humans. Think of the realm where we live as like the inside of a huge domed stadium with a semi-transparent roof through which we can see the heavenly bodies on the other side. When biblical authors mention the windows of heaven, they are imagining openings in the roof that can allow water to come down in the form of rain onto what they picture as a flat earth. Below the earth they picture more water, as well as the realm of *Sheol* where the dead survive in some very diminished form. The view of the world taken for granted by biblical authors is one they share with other Near Eastern cultures of the time, as can be seen from the creation stories of those other cultures.

So, when a biblical author gives an account of creation, it is in terms of a picture of the natural order that the biblical author and the audience of that time period share, but we do not. When we read Gen 1, we come to the text with a different understanding of what the world is like, which we have acquired from the science of a later era. We don't picture things in terms of a three-story universe composed of the heavens above, the earth beneath, and the underworld. So, if we take the biblical author to be used by God to reveal something to us, we have to try to put the message into a form that fits with our view of the world. In other words, we have to distinguish the cultural clothing that shapes the message from the revelation that is expressed through that clothing.[1]

Failing to make this distinction leads to misguided ways of understanding the Bible that are displayed when people wrestle with the question

---

1. Parallel to differences with ancient authors about matters we label scientific are differences in the way we represent metaphysical realities. In the New Testament the conflict with evil is described in terms of encountering evil spirits who sometimes possess human beings. Just as we can take biblical messages seriously without adopting ancient scientific ideas, we can read biblical references to evil spirits as a culturally shaped way of talking about the reality of evil. John and Harvey Walton say that we should take biblical descriptions of evil spirits not as teachings about the nature of the spiritual realm, but as references to accounts that would have been assumed by ancient audiences. See *Demons and Spirits*, 16–18. Victor White suggests that when biblical writers speak of casting out demons, they are describing what Jungian psychologists would call "unassimilated autonomous complexes" in a "different language." See *God and the Unconscious*, 189. Walter Wink in numerous books connects biblical language about demonic powers to systems that structure human life, which have what he calls a "spiritual aspect" that can dominate us. See, for example, *Powers That Be*, 4.

of whether what the text says about the nature of the universe can be harmonized with the claims of science. Some people conclude that because they cannot fit the biblical account and science together, scientific claims about such matters as biological evolution or the age of the earth have to be rejected. But the same sort of mistake can be made by those who accept what science says. In relation to the creation story of Gen 1, I have heard people ask questions such as, "Could the days be long periods rather than literal twenty-four-hour days?" In asking this question, they are trying to make the Genesis account consistent with their own scientific understanding of a long process through which our world is formed. The suggestion is that the account fits with our science, even if the harmony is not immediately obvious. However, when we try to read the biblical account in a way that fits with our science, we are treating the text as if it addresses issues that it does not address. The author is describing creation in terms that would have made sense to people in the ancient world who did not think in terms of the accounts offered by our science.

When we acknowledge that the biblical story is told in a form that fits with the understanding of the natural world predominant at the time, we are in a better position to consider what the text says to us. If this story is to make sense to us, it won't be because it satisfies our scientific curiosity about how things came to be. It will be because we, along with the biblical writer, raise the question of the purpose of the natural order in which we find ourselves and are receptive to answering that question in terms of a Creator who put such an order in place. The biblical account is an affirmation of faith that the God Israel has experienced historically is the one who has ordered the world to produce a habitation that is suitable for human life. More than that, it is an affirmation that none of the gods worshiped by other nations have a power that can rival this Creator.

Scholarly study of the Bible gives us reason to think that the account of creation in Gen 1 was given its final shape by Israelite priests during or shortly after the time of the Babylonian exile.[2] It is noteworthy that the story is told in terms of days of the Hebrew week. Each day begins at sunset, with the seventh day being Israel's Sabbath, a day of special importance for those with priestly duties. Like the prophets of the time, these priests must have struggled with the question of why God had allowed the disaster of a foreign power destroying the city of Jerusalem, including the temple, which was conceived as Yahweh's dwelling place. As these priests edit the accounts of the nation's history available to them, they interpret that history as showing

---

2. There are many good biblical introductions that discuss sources of the text. For an account of sources in the book of Genesis, see Carr, *Reading Genesis*, 3–22.

the exile is a result of Israel's idolatrous worship of other gods. Nevertheless, they retain a hope that somehow the God Israel has betrayed will at some point restore the nation. When they shape the accounts of national origins and history into their final form, they place the creation account of Gen 1 as a preamble to the rest of the story.

In the late nineteenth century archaeologists discovered clay tablets with other creation stories from the ancient Near East. When scholars studied these stories, it was apparent to them that there were similarities to the biblical account.[3] All these stories seemed to share a common way of thinking about creation, such as the idea of an initial watery chaos that is brought under control. It seems plausible to think that the writers of the Gen 1 account knew about stories of other nations. In fact, there is some reason to suspect that their own account is formulated as a kind of response to the now well-known Babylonian story that portrays creation as occurring after a power struggle between multiple gods. These priestly writers have the audacity to proclaim in their story that the heavenly bodies the Babylonians identified with deities are all produced by and under the control of the one Creator who has the power to speak things into existence. The claim is audacious in part because we are talking about a conquered people proclaiming that the deity they worship is the real power. Later Hebrews will recognize these texts as authoritative expressions of the faith of Israel.

THE BIBLE AS REVELATION

How can the Bible be a revelation from God if it comes to us in the form of writings by human authors whose understanding is shaped by the views of a particular time and place, some of which we think are mistaken? Part of the answer to this question is that we can sometimes distinguish between the fundamental message and the form in which the message is expressed. So, for example, we can say that while the ancient writer was describing things in terms of the understanding of the natural world that people of the time had, the fundamental message is about God's production and maintenance of the natural order.

However, taking the Bible to be a revelation from God is more complicated than filtering out ancient scientific claims and finding an underlying theological message. In the first place, it is not just science that reveals our differences with the ancient authors of biblical texts. These writers presume

---

3. Any good Old Testament survey will offer comparisons between Genesis accounts and other ancient Near Eastern accounts. For an introduction to this issue, see Clifford, *Creation Accounts*.

a range of ideas that would have seemed obvious in their cultural setting, but seem alien to us. If we try to filter out ideas that are unacceptable, what we will be filtering out includes not just peripheral matters. Some of their ethical and theological views are unacceptable to us.

Consider, for example, the fundamental issue of whether there is one God. I remember being puzzled as a child by one of the ten commandments: "you shall have no other gods before me" (Exod 20:3). I wondered whether the command was suggesting that there was more than one god. I had been taught, of course, that there was only one God, but if so, why should there be a command that referred to other gods? The typical interpretation I heard in church was to understand the term "god" metaphorically. A god, we were told, is whatever we give first priority to. So, we might make a god out of money or security or power or pleasure. I don't deny the legitimacy of this sort of lesson, but it tends to hide from us the question of how the original recipients of the command would have understood it.

There is convincing evidence that the early Israelites were not monotheists, but what scholars call *henotheists*. That is, they accepted the existence of multiple deities, but gave their allegiance to a particular one. The command to have no other gods directed them to give exclusive allegiance to Yahweh who had brought them into existence as a people. As far as Israel was concerned, Yahweh was the deity for them to worship, not any of the other gods. The subsequent history told in scriptural texts reveals how difficult Israelites found it to keep the command to have no other gods before Yahweh. They were constantly tempted to seek out other deities. We can imagine an Israelite living in the promised land thinking that Yahweh may be great for fighting battles, but wondering what Yahweh knows about raising crops. The temptation was to hedge their bets by worshiping an agricultural deity, such as Asherah, along with Yahweh. We may have difficulty wrapping our heads around the idea, but the demands of exclusive worship were difficult because people of the time regarded the other gods as real powers who could bestow benefits, even if Yahweh was greater than the others.

Most biblical scholars think that Israel becomes firmly monotheistic only around the time of the Babylonian exile. Only then do their prophets and priests affirm clearly that there are no other gods. However, the Hebrew Scriptures include written accounts deriving from oral traditions that come from periods well before the nation became unequivocally monotheistic. So, when we read some parts of the Bible, we are dealing with texts by authors who affirm the priority of Yahweh, but assume the existence of other deities. In other words, they portray a view of things that we would judge deficient in relation to a full-fledged monotheism.

But if God is the source of biblical revelation, how can that revelation include deficient ideas? Two considerations are helpful in answering this question. First, we should recognize that what can be revealed at any particular point in time needs to come in terms that people of that time and place can comprehend. But what will make sense to the people of one time and place may be deficient in relation to a fuller understanding. Second, we should think of biblical revelation as a gradual process. We can posit that God accepts the limits of human capacity, but attempts over time to nudge people closer to the truth. So, for example, people who think of deity in polytheistic terms may not be ready for the thought that there is only one God, but they may be able to comprehend the idea of one god having a special relationship with the nation and demanding absolute allegiance. Eventually, subsequent generations may be prepared to recognize that there are no other gods.

What I am describing can be put in terms that are familiar to theologians. Since the time of the early church fathers, Christian thinkers have taught that revelation involves *divine accommodation*.[4] That is, God's communication with human beings is adapted to a form that humans can understand, and what we can understand at any point in time may be fairly distant from the full truth. The church fathers sometimes used the analogy of communicating something to a child that was beyond the child's ability to fully comprehend. Note that communication may be adequate for some purposes, even if it falls short of a conveying a more mature grasp of things. Historically, Christian thinkers who accepted this idea tended to think of God as working with the biblical author to adapt some message that the author understood to an audience that lacked the capacity to receive that message. My account of divine accommodation, however, follows contemporary theologians who think of the biblical authors themselves as finite human beings whose writing reflects their own limited understanding.

To accept such an idea means recognizing that what the human author says may be deficient from the perspective of someone with a greater grasp of the truth. We can acknowledge as much, but still affirm that this author participates in a process that over time leads to fuller truth. The idea of a process that leads over time to fuller truth is what theologians have called *progressive revelation*. The concept of divine accommodation helps to explain why divine revelation needs to be progressive. What can be understood at any given point may be limited, but we can conceive of God building on earlier ideas to prepare for a fuller understanding later.

---

4. Sparks, *God's Word in Human Words*, 236–42.

Combining the concept of divine accommodation with the concept of progressive revelation has implications for how we should interpret Scripture. Most of us can point to particular Bible passages that we think of as high points of divine revelation. When we read parts of the Bible that seem more problematic, we tend to correct them in the light of our understanding of the more adequate truth we believe we find in the Bible's high points. Consider, for example, the Psalms. There are quite a few Psalms that focus on complaints about enemies. The Psalmist prays that terrible things will happen to enemies, including having their babies' brains bashed out on rocks (Ps 137:9). We can recognize that such hateful attitudes are not totally absent from our own reaction to those who wrong us. But while the authors of these Psalms probably thought of their revengeful attitudes as perfectly legitimate, likely even coinciding with God's attitudes, we evaluate them as deficient in the light of Jesus's teaching to love our enemies. We are even a bit embarrassed by such passages and tend to omit them in public Scripture reading on Sunday morning.

The early church fathers had a different way of dealing with scriptural texts they considered problematic. They read them as having a higher-level meaning that should be substituted for the literal meaning. Augustine advocates the view that when you can't take a scriptural passage literally, you should find some allegorical way of reading it that makes it acceptable. So, for example, he took the infants of Babylon whose brains the biblical writer wanted bashed out to represent the evil desires of people and not literal babies.[5] While we can recognize symbolic meanings, modern people are less inclined to simply disregard the more obvious surface meanings. But if we don't resort to allegory, we need ways of demoting understandings that seem to us deficient in the light of what we take to be higher expressions of the biblical message.

I acknowledge the kind of biblical interpretation that allows us to reject some of what we find in the Bible as inconsistent with more fundamental teachings or fuller revelation involves judgment. We can often be fairly confident about some judgments. For example, we are more confident of the teaching that God is love than we are of any passage that portrays God as acting in cruel and vindictive ways. However, we should not assume the viewpoints from which we judge are uninfected by inadequate assumptions from our own cultural setting. While there is no viable alternative to making judgments, we should acknowledge that we can get things wrong. Fortunately, however, the Bible often seems very clear about the things we most

---

5. Augustine, *Expositions on the Psalms*, 632.

need to get right. The question of whether we should love our neighbor, for example, is not up for grabs.

We might wish that we could just identify the message of each biblical author with God's message for us, but we cannot. We need to distinguish between what the human author is saying and what God might be saying to us through that human author. Reading the Bible is like listening in on conversations where the authors had particular messages for people of the time. As we listen in, we pay attention to what the message might have been for its contemporaneous recipients. But we also think about what it might mean for us in the light of how our community of faith has understood the fuller revelation. In that light we sometimes judge that what the human author says is not God's message for us. The rest of the revelatory story allows us to correct some perspectives that we can recognize as defective. Nevertheless, sometimes listening in on a particular conversation from the past, even one we have reason to question in various respects, challenges our own partial and finite viewpoints. Sometimes through these conversations we hear the word of God for us in unexpected ways.

CHAPTER 5

Disturbing Portrayals of God

SUPPOSE THAT YOU READ from a reliable source about a warlike tribe that has been systematically conquering villages in a far-away country that lacks a strong central authority. People of this tribe have an antagonistic attitude toward anyone who is different from them, ethnically or religiously. In some cases, they go into another village and offer terms of peace. The village can accept enslavement of their population or they can try to resist. If they fight, all their men will be killed, and the younger females will be given to male soldiers as spoils of war. In other cases, the tribe offers no peace treaty, but overruns the village and slaughters all men, women, children, and animals. They justify the extermination of entire populations on the grounds that these aliens have gods different from their own and that leaving any of them alive could endanger the purity of their own tribe's religion. This tribe claims that their god has given them the land where these other people live and ordered the extermination of all who resist their conquest. They say that their deity has specifically told them to show no mercy toward those they attack.

My guess is that you might be enraged by the brutality of this tribe. You might condemn it, using terms such as genocide or barbarism. Even if you think that war can be justified under some circumstances, you would be appalled at the unprovoked attacks and indiscriminate slaughter of civilians, and you would likely regard the religious claims made in support of this violence as self-serving rationalization. Perhaps you would support sending an international force to stop the bloodshed, and you might send money to organizations that provide aid for those who have fled the violence. At any rate, you would not be inclined to take seriously the claims that the tribe's conquests are justified because the deity they worship has commanded them to do what they are doing.

What I have described this tribe as doing is pretty much the way we are told in the Bible that the Israelites were instructed to behave toward the populations they encountered as they invaded the land of Canaan. The Hebrew Scriptures tell us that God not only approved these kinds of actions, but ordered them. In fact, according to the accounts, God was sometimes angry when people from Canaanite towns were left alive or even when some of their property was not destroyed.

The texts distinguish between what is to be done in the promised land and outside it. In Deut 20 the instructions to Israelites about attacks outside the promised land are:

> When you draw near to a town to fight against it, offer it terms of peace. If it accepts your terms of peace and surrenders to you, then all the people in it shall serve you at forced labor. If it does not submit to you peacefully, but makes war against you, then you shall besiege it; and when the Lord your God gives it into your hand, you shall put all its males to the sword. You may, however, take as your booty the women, the children, livestock, and everything else in the town, all its spoil . . . (Deut 20:10–14).

However, in the promised land they are told to make no peace treaty and show no mercy: "you must not let anything that breathes remain alive. You shall annihilate them . . . so that they may not teach you to do all the abhorrent things that they do for their gods . . ." (Deut 20:16–18). Similar instructions are repeated multiple times in Hebrew Scripture.

Some people react differently when events of this kind are described in the Bible than they would if they heard about them on the evening news. Some Christians say that when this sort of violence is authorized by God, it is acceptable. Some defend it on the grounds that we can't judge God by human standards. Some claim that the extermination of indigenous populations was justified because the people attacked were especially evil or because there was too great a risk that Israelites would be tempted to idol worship. Some Christians are uncomfortable with the kinds of things attributed to God, but assume that somehow there must be a good reason.

I am not persuaded by attempts to provide moral defenses for what God is said to command. It is difficult to think that the kind of deity who seems to care so little about the lives of non-Israelites can be identified with the God who loves the whole world. But the account of God as ordering the violence and participating in it is clearly in the Bible, and some people have reasoned that anyone who accepts the Bible as divine revelation just has to believe what the text says. Since biblical accounts come from God, they say, those accounts must be true.

I suggest we need to think about biblical revelation differently. It is understandable why someone might believe that if God is going to reveal something, then the revelation must be completely true. However, I think this way of conceiving the matter comes from *an overly simple picture of how God might communicate with human beings.* If we try to conceive of a message that comes from God, we need to recognize that communication involves a recipient as well as a sender. What can be communicated depends to a great extent on the capacity of the recipient to comprehend a message. So, God as a communicator, might be limited when trying to communicate with people whose understanding is shaped by the cultural frame of reference of a particular time and place. The relevant theological term here is *divine accommodation.* I used this concept in the last chapter to explain how we can accept the Bible as revelation without accepting some things biblical authors assumed to be true. The idea is that whatever God reveals has to make sense to people using the concepts and assumptions of their time. Some people think of divine accommodation as God sending a message that is dumbed down enough to be understood. I prefer to think in terms of the communication passing through a medium that may distort it.

Have you ever been in a conversation where the other person could not take seriously what you were saying because that person assumed things you thought were just wrong or they had a store of beliefs and paradigms you regarded as oversimplifications or confusions? In such conversations people often end up talking past each other. You may imagine that if you could just give the other person the right facts, there would be a meeting of the minds. But often there is not a meeting of the minds because the other person is starting from a place that is very different from the place you occupy. Sometimes the starting points are so different that it doesn't even seem worth the effort. Genuine communication would take considerable good will on both sides, and it would also take a very long time.

So, imagine God trying to communicate with people from an ancient culture who have ways of thinking that shape their understanding of whatever God wants to communicate. If we try to imagine what communication of this sort might be like, we should be able to see why what comes through may sometimes be garbled and confused, but might nevertheless be a step on the way to fuller understanding. Improved understanding of some matters might take generations. In the last chapter I used the term *progressive revelation* to describe a process that moves gradually from a limited beginning toward fuller truth. But if revelation is progressive, some parts of the Bible are closer to the truth than others.

So, how does all this apply to biblical accounts that represent God as a warrior deity who intervenes on behalf of Israel and treats Israel's enemies with ruthless disregard? I suggest that we are dealing with an ancient people who are trying to make sense of an encounter with God in the terms available to them. The ways they had for thinking about deities turn out to be similar to the ways their Middle Eastern neighbors thought. The religions of these tribes assume a deity who fights for their tribe and in opposition to other tribes. In this way of thinking, it is important to be connected to a god who is powerful. If you win your battles and take over another group's territory, your success is seen as a sign that your god is stronger than the other group's god. If you can utterly wipe out your enemy, the result may be seen as credit to your god.[1] Israel is not unique in presuming the acceptability of war that involves total extermination of their enemies. Their neighbors accepted the practice as well. Israelites thought of this kind of warfare as a way of glorifying their god because that is what all tribal cultures in the vicinity during that time period assumed.

What then should we say about biblical portrayals of God acting in ways we find profoundly disturbing? I say we should think of these portrayals as coming to us through the lens of a way of understanding things that we don't share. We can comprehend why biblical writers of the time might have thought that God commanded them to show no mercy and kill all the people in a neighboring village. They thought in terms of the prevailing view of their time about how these things worked. But understanding why they might have thought as they did does not mean that we have to endorse their view or agree that God endorsed it. We can look at what we take to be a more primitive conception of what God desires in the light of what we believe to be a fuller understanding of God's nature and say God did not command those atrocities, even though biblical writers thought Israel received such commands.

There are sincere people who cannot accept the account I am giving because I am saying that the Bible can say things that are wrong. Some of these people accept the idea of progressive revelation, but draw the line at saying that less complete forms of revelation can be mistaken. For them it is axiomatic that whatever the Bible says is true. Hence, if the Bible says God commanded extermination of all men, women, and children, following such a command must have been the right thing to do. I can see why someone would be reluctant to admit that some things the Bible says should be judged false. But I think that we have to put up with an extraordinary level of cognitive dissonance to hold that while God commanded things that

---

1. Enns, *How the Bible Works*, 144–49; Boyd, *Cross Vision*, 121–32.

strike us as monstrously evil, God is nevertheless perfectly good and worthy of our worship. It is better in my judgment to think that because revelation has to fit with the limited understanding available to recipients at the time and place it is written, what comes across can take a form that is seriously flawed. Biblical authors who are not yet in a position to grasp much of what God ultimately wants to reveal may say things that we reject because they conflict with the fuller biblical revelation that culminates in Christ.

BIBLICAL ANTHROPOMORPHISM

Someone who thinks that if the Bible says it, you can't disagree with it is probably disregarding the extent to which his or her own readings of biblical texts diverge from what the texts say. I want to illustrate my claim about how people read the Bible in relation to accounts that describe God in ways that strike modern readers as excessively anthropomorphic. That is, I am calling attention to biblical passages in which God is described as having characteristics modeled on human characteristics, which are noticeable because the descriptions project human imperfections onto God.[2]

Before we look at the Bible, consider anthropomorphism in a nonbiblical source. One of the immediate impressions we get from stories about the gods of Greek polytheistic religions is how human these gods seem. To be sure, they have powers that go beyond what humans can do, but their motivations strike us as all too human. According to the stories, they are driven by emotions such as jealousy, anger, and lust that remind us of our own failings. They may occasionally do admirable things, but they regularly display the kinds of vices that we condemn in each other. It is hard to avoid thinking that humans have created these gods in their own image, making them superior in power, but projecting on them the same kinds of moral weaknesses that humans exhibit.

If we don't look attentively at biblical texts, we may assume that the deity described in these texts is free from projected human weaknesses. Nevertheless, some biblical stories of God's behavior are uncomfortably reminiscent of the kinds of human frailties that stand out in the stories of polytheistic religions. Consider, for example, an account from Exod 32. God is portrayed as angry with the people of Israel. While Moses was on the mountain receiving the commandments, the people made themselves an idol in the shape of a calf, bowing down and offering sacrifices to this idol. According to the account, God is enraged and proposes to let this anger

---

2. See my chapter "Anthropomorphism and Mystery" in *Meaning and Mystery*, 109–28.

intensify to a point where the people of Israel will be destroyed. The plan is that God will start over and form a new nation beginning with Moses. Then something startling happens. Moses proceeds to talk God down from this angry response, suggesting that it will give the Egyptians license to say that God has acted with an evil intent in rescuing the people, only to destroy them. Moses also reminds God of the promises made to Abraham, Isaac, and Jacob. As a result of the intercession of Moses, God is persuaded to revoke the threat to destroy the Israelites. The text says, "And the Lord changed his mind about the disaster that he planned to bring on his people" (Exod 32:14).

If we take the text at face value, what we see is a portrayal of God as subject to fits of anger leading to rash decisions and in need of calming down to think more rationally about the consequences. In this portrayal, God seems either not to know some things or is not attentive to them. However, Jewish and Christian interpreters in later times don't read the text in this way. They take for granted an understanding of God as free of imperfections and human weaknesses, which leads them to discount overly anthropomorphic portrayals, such as the idea that God throws temper tantrums or acts rashly without full consideration of relevant information. The application of what we might call *control beliefs* about God derived from the tradition's subsequent critique of anthropomorphism functions more or less automatically to shape how modern interpreters understand such accounts. Those of us who have internalized a more reflective understanding of God don't seriously entertain conceptions of God that we consider unworthy. Nevertheless, it is hard to avoid concluding that the writers of some biblical accounts really thought of God in the anthropomorphic ways described in the text that we regard as unacceptable.

My point here is that people with some understanding of Jewish or Christian theological tradition more or less automatically discount things the text says that conflict with reflective conclusions about God's nature the tradition comes to later. It is possible, I suppose, to posit that the biblical writers didn't really believe the anthropomorphic portrayals of God, but described God that way for dramatic purposes, but when we examine the texts without presuming the writer must believe as we do, it seems more plausible to conclude the writer had a more primitive view of God than the view we have learned to accept. We treat the descriptions as metaphorical ways of speaking about God. But that way of reading things does not come from the text itself.

Some Christians worry that if we think we can pronounce what some biblical text says to be false, then we can just reject anything we don't like. I don't think that the problem is as big as they imagine. We can reject some things on the basis of what we take to be truths that the biblical tradition as a whole gives us strong reason to affirm. Hence, for example, we reject behaviors ascribed to God that do not fit with the God revealed in the life and teaching of Jesus. In doing so, we are saying that what we judge to be a fuller revelation gives us a basis for rejecting what seems deficient in relation to it. We are not saying that one can simply decide what to accept or reject on the basis of personal preferences.

PLACES TO STAND

Interpreting the Bible in the way I am suggesting involves having some places where we think that we get closer to the heart of revelatory truth. We may not agree about all those places, but I suspect that we agree about many of them. For example, I think most of us agree with the prophetic critique of the Jewish sacrificial system. When the prophets say things like, "What does the Lord require of you, but to do justice, to love mercy, and to walk humbly with your God?" (Micah 6:8), it seems to many of us that they cut to the heart of the matter. Ritual exercises have a point, but God's deeper concern is that we treat each other well and remember our place within a larger scheme of things. When Jesus was asked to sum up the Jewish law, he repeated the scriptural commands to love God first of all and to love your neighbor as yourself. Summing up things in such a way provides a kind of principle that helps us distinguish matters of central importance from lesser concerns.

I think we can also say that when Paul asserts that "God was in Christ reconciling the world unto himself" (2 Cor 5:19), we have a high point in biblical revelation. The events of Jesus's life, death, and resurrection, including what Jesus taught, show us what God is like and what God is trying to do in the world. But when we affirm that Jesus shows us what God is like or that what Jesus taught shows us what we need to be, we have to judge as deficient ways of thinking about what God is like or what we should be that don't fit with this understanding. In doing so, we are not ignoring biblical revelation, but being faithful to its progressive nature.

I am not denying that interpreting the Bible in this way involves judgment, nor am I denying that our judgments can be incorrect. But I think that our concern with having a guaranteed way of avoiding all mistakes is obsessive and misguided. We can be wrong about a great many things, just as I have claimed that biblical authors were sometimes wrong. We too approach biblical revelation from cultural assumptions of our own place and time. We can't claim to be free of blind spots or to have the kind of absolute certainty about everything that some Christians aspire to have.

Nevertheless, we can have some places where we take a firm stand with a high degree of confidence. Because I read the rest of the Bible in the light of what I take to be the fullest revelation of God in Jesus, I am much more confident that God wants us to love our enemies than I am of reports that God approves of ruthless violence against those we oppose. I am more confident that the nature of God is more fully revealed when Jesus prays for those who brought about his death than when people in the Psalms cry out that their enemies should receive the cruelest vengeance. I am more confident that God is on the side of victims of oppression than on the side of those who think that military power gives them the right to oppress. All of these are judgments, but some judgments seem to get closer to the heart of what God wants to communicate to us.

Does it really make a difference if you think God approves of and participates in coercive violence against those who are too weak to resist? I suspect it makes a difference in whether you can genuinely love God, or just pretend you do. I suspect it also makes a difference with regard to what you think it is legitimate for you to do. Some historically horrendous acts have been carried out by people who assumed they had biblical authorization for acting as they did. People who subdue others by violent means often think they are doing just what God would approve of. They are in effect imitating the kind of God they believe in.

It is not just in the conquest of Canaan that we find disturbing accounts of God. There are accounts of God behaving in unworthy ways throughout the Bible. Some atheists say that they cannot believe in the biblical God precisely because of the despicable behavior attributed to God in the Bible. They have a point. But an alternative to rejecting the biblical God is to say that some of the portrayals of God in the Bible are mistaken. Just as we recognize that God is sometimes portrayed in overly anthropomorphic ways that might have seemed natural in the thought world of the time, we can recognize that portrayals of God acting in ways that parallel human immorality are also products of what might have seemed natural within the thought world of some biblical writers. However, in the light of fuller revelation, particularly the revelation of God in Christ, we can look at such accounts and say, "God would not do such a thing." If we have reason to think that God is more accurately revealed in Christ, we have reason to reject accounts that conflict with that revelation, even if we find them in the Bible.

CHAPTER 6

Misplaced Expectations

IMAGINE COMING INTO A room where your uncle is telling a story that is the focus of everyone's attention. His story has been going on for a while, and he is apparently describing something that happened to him. The story seems a bit fantastic, but you are well aware of your uncle's tendency to exaggerate and dramatize events to make them more interesting. Even though you sometimes roll your eyes when he says something outrageous, you can't help but admire his skill at composing a tale. Something that would not seem worth describing if it happened to you might be for him the basis of a captivating narrative. You have observed that some of his stories change over time, and it is often interesting when he puts a new twist on old material. When you were younger, you assumed that all the events in his stories were described just as they happened, but your relatives clued you in on what to expect from your uncle. You have learned to take some of what he says "with a grain of salt," but you have also frequently discovered that his stories show deep insight into things you hadn't thought about. On this occasion, however, the story seems odd in a way you can't quite put your finger on. It is only when he gets to the punchline that you realize that your uncle is telling a joke.

Knowing how to interpret oral or written messages depends on identifying the type of communication we are receiving. Is it a scientific explanation? Is it a historical narrative? Is it a made-for-TV dramatization of a story from the news? Is it a tall tale? Is it intended ironically? Is it a way of flirting? Is it a joke? We learn to make such assessments quickly and often without explicit thought. We can misconstrue things, of course, such as failing to recognize that a remark is intended sarcastically, but when we are dealing with familiar types of communication, we are usually able to correctly assess what is going on. However, the potential for misunderstanding is magnified when we find ourselves dealing with communications that don't quite fit into familiar categories.

It may be surprising to some, but dealing with unfamiliar types of writing is a central task we face when we read the Bible. Biblical authors wrote in the context of cultures whose types of writing don't correspond exactly to our own. They followed literary conventions that were commonly accepted in their time but differ from what we are used to. Unless we are careful, we can approach these writings with expectations from our own setting that result in misunderstandings. We can presume, for example, that a biblical story provides a documentary-like account of events when what is offered is more like a creative dramatization. We can mistakenly imagine that an ancient genealogy is like what we might seek to produce when we try to trace our ancestors. We can fail to recognize clues that indicate ancient poetry or ancient methods of storytelling. Many of the problems we find in biblical texts arise when we fail to correctly identify the kind of material we are dealing with. Some of these problems would disappear altogether and others would be significantly mitigated, if we could let go of our misplaced expectations. In this chapter my focus will be on misplaced expectations about the historical accuracy of biblical texts.

FICTION IN THE BIBLE

In the churches where I grew up, the presumption was that biblical stories tell us exactly what happened with the kind of accuracy we might get from an audio/video recording of events. However, this view is far too simple. In the first place, some biblical accounts should be understood as fiction. The book of Jonah is an example. The book deals with the mission of a Jewish prophet to the city of Nineveh, capital of the ancient Assyrian empire. The Assyrians were known in the ancient world as brutal warriors whose reputation for ruthless cruelty evoked terror in other nations. Assyria conquered and destroyed the northern Jewish kingdom (Israel) in 722 BCE, and they were a constant threat to the southern kingdom (Judah) during the next century until Nineveh fell to the Babylonians in 612 BCE.

The book of Jonah was written after the Babylonian exile (586 to 538 BCE) when Assyrian power was a thing of the distant past. The writer sets the story during the time of Assyrian dominance. According to the account, a Hebrew prophet named Jonah is commissioned by God to go and deliver a message to the people of Nineveh that God is about to destroy the city because of its wickedness. For obvious reasons, Jonah does not want to go, but his efforts to run away prove futile. Jonah eventually goes around the city delivering his message of judgment, and amazingly the Assyrians from the king on down repent of their wicked ways. Jonah is not pleased when God calls off the predicted punishment. The moral of the story is that the God of Israel cares not just for the Jewish people, but has compassion and mercy even for their worst enemies.

This book is a wonderful story with an uplifting teaching about God. It is clearly written to make a point. Just as clearly, there is good reason to think it is a work of creative fiction. First, the account of Jonah being swallowed by a fish and then surviving after the fish spits him up three days later would likely have been recognized by ancient audiences as a clear indication that what is related is not history.[1] More importantly, the climactic event reported in the book—Assyria mending her ways because of a visit from a Hebrew prophet—would have left historical traces if it had actually happened. But there is no such evidence. The author is presumably not expecting an audience from the postexilic period to believe that these events did happen, but is using the story to teach a lesson about the nature of God. It is a kind of "what if" story that picks out a very unpopular candidate for God's compassion in order to challenge those who think of Yahweh in purely nationalistic terms and ignore parts of the Hebrew Scriptures indicating that Israel's mission is to bless the whole world.

I can't see that it diminishes the book of Jonah to say the events reported in it are not historical. Surely divine revelation can occur through works of creative fiction. Isn't that precisely what happens in the parables of Jesus? Though I won't go into it, I'll suggest that the books of Job and Esther also fall into the category of fiction. They don't record historical events, but they do present significant theological messages in dramatic form. We should be disappointed about their historical content only if we have the mistaken expectation that they should be read as history.

GENESIS 1–11

Scholars have long noted similarities between the creation and flood stories found in Genesis and the stories of other ancient Near Eastern nations. In the case of flood stories there are similarities of detail too great to be regarded as coincidence. To be sure, there are differences between the accounts we find in Genesis and accounts from other nations in the Near East. For example, the Babylonians told a story in which creation follows a violent struggle

---

1. Enns, *How the Bible Actually Works*, 105.

between the gods from which one god emerges as victorious. In Genesis the created order is portrayed as the work of a single deity whose power is uncontested. Genesis also represents the purposes of God and the role of human beings differently from the ways they are portrayed in other Near Eastern accounts. The differences are important, but so are the similarities. All of these stories show signs of common ways of thinking that ancient people of this region shared, but differ from our own ways of thinking.

For example, people of our era tend to associate creation with the origin of matter that makes up the universe. In the ancient Near East creation was thought of primarily in terms of bringing order to chaos.[2] Their creation stories start with a watery chaos that is somehow tamed. In Genesis God separates the waters above the earth and the waters below the earth from our realm to make a habitat suitable for animal and human life. A corollary of thinking of creation as bringing order from disorder is to view it as a continuing activity. In an ancient Near Eastern context chaos is viewed as a constant threat that the gods need to deal with. In biblical thought God is understood as continuing to keep the forces that generate disorder under control.

At a more general level than these common ways of thinking, we can notice a common explanatory style the ancients had that differs from the ways we explain things. In prescientific cultures explanations about ultimate matters took the form of stories. For them the most satisfying accounts of origins would not have been in terms of natural forces, but in terms of the kinds of drama we find in the human world. So, if you think gods are the highest reality, you need to tell stories about what the gods do that results in a created order. If you believe God is the ultimate source, you need to tell a story about what God does. Scholars sometimes refer to stories of this type about ultimate origins as myths. The term can be misleading if we think of myths only as false stories. The stories in question are ways of representing truths about reality by people who did not think in terms of our kind of scientific explanations.[3] If we don't read them as attempts to give a play-by-play account of long-ago events, we are in a better position to understand the kinds of truths they convey.

For many people, the all-important question is whether the events portrayed in biblical stories actually happened. Was there really a first man and a first woman who lived in a garden? Did God repent of making human beings and send a flood that wiped out almost all human and animal life? Did God restrict the length of human life because of illicit relations between

---

2. Walton, *Old Testament Theology*, 71–84.
3. Enns, *Inspiration and Incarnation*, 39.

heavenly beings and human females? Did the diversity of human languages result from a misguided project of building a tower that could reach heaven? If we think of Israelite stories as like the stories other nations told, we have some reason to think that such questions are misguided. Like other ancient peoples, Israelites could construct stories of what might have happened, given their beliefs about God. They could describe how an idyllic existence was disrupted by human disobedience, how God attempts to rescue human beings from the consequences of their misdirected passions, how all of these events set the stage for the climatic act of calling Abraham to establish a new nation. Like the stories of other nations, these Israelite stories show the signs of being works of creative dramatization.

It might be said that God could reveal what happened between the beginning of things and the establishment of the nation. Some people think the early chapters of Genesis contain such a revelation and should be read as a detailed record of what happened before recorded history. They believe the biblical stories of creation and flood and towers built to reach the heavens are all depictions of events that someone with the available technology who had been present might have recorded with a video camera. Some people take seriously the idea that Noah's Ark might be found some day through an archeological expedition to the mountains of Turkey.

I think attempts to view Gen 1–11 as providing a historical record of primordial events is misguided. It is not a matter of thinking that God could not reveal such things. It is more a matter of thinking that in viewing these stories as historical, we are putting them in the wrong genre. Consider one example. When we look at the account in Gen 2 about the first humans, we find a story that if we had encountered it in any other context, we might put in a category of stories that begin with words like "once upon a time." When the story introduces talking serpents and magic trees, our first thought should not be that we are dealing with straightforward history. Rather, we should suspect that we are dealing with a work of creative imagination that aims at a different type of truth. When we read this story and the other stories in the first eleven chapters of Genesis as like the stories other nations told to present a narrative version of their picture of the world, we discover more plausible ways of understanding these accounts.

While it strains our credulity to read these texts as history, we can appreciate how ancient people made sense of things through narratives of this kind, and we can see how the authors of biblical texts have used the literary forms and the source material available to them to give a narrative explication of Israel's core beliefs about God and human life. In other words, we can distinguish between "narratives that use real events in the human world as their referents" and "narratives that use perceived cosmological reality as their referent."[4] We can also find that entering into the story world of these ancient texts can stimulate our own thinking about who God is and what God is doing in the world.

BIBLICAL WRITING ABOUT THE PAST

Even when a biblical text deals with historical events, we should not suppose that the writing is history, as we understand the term. Our ideas of history are themselves a development of a culture that has come to prize accumulating and objectively interpreting the weight of evidence. We expect historians to be able to assess the likelihood of purported events in the light of the documentary material they have available. Of course, we recognize there is constructive work by historians, but we expect their constructive efforts to be constrained by what the available evidence supports. If historians offer speculative hypotheses, we expect these hypotheses to be acknowledged as such.

According to most scholars, this type of historical writing did not exist in the ancient world. There were, of course, reports of events, but these reports typically display overriding concerns that are treated as more important than the concern to get at what actually happened. For example, some ancient writings are in service of the king.[5] While they may contain accurate reports of events, we can recognize that the main purpose of documents authorized by the royal establishment was to make the king look good. We might compare these writings to the messages of a Communications Director for a political official. Such a person seeks to spin the facts in such a way that the narrative reflects well on the boss. Some ancient writings of this sort include outright falsifications, including reports of military victories that were really defeats.

Biblical accounts of Israel's kings do not generally aim at this kind of royal aggrandizement. In fact, they are often very critical of the kings. But like other historical accounts from the ancient world, they are written for purposes other than producing an accurate record of events. The authors of biblical histories are primarily concerned to tell the national story in a way that answers vital questions about Israel's identity and destiny. In the accounts of Samuel through Kings bad things that have befallen the nation are portrayed as results of repeated failures to fulfill covenant responsibilities, especially the command not to worship gods other than Yahweh. The kings of Israel and Judah are singled out for strong condemnation for failing

---

4. Walton, *Old Testament Theology*, 83.
5. Sparks, *God's Word in Human Words*, 63–66.

to lead the nation in obedience to God's commands. In other words, biblical authors offer an account of events that is shaped by a recognizable theological interpretation of what happened. If we think of what they are doing as like what other ancient writers do, we can sometimes judge that narratives of particular events are ways of making theological points that are not always closely connected to what happened.[6]

The process of writing down the nation's story began during the settled period when Israel was ruled by kings, and the great bulk of writing about the past in Hebrew Scripture deals with the time of the monarchy and its aftermath. However, Israel also begins during this period to reflect on and write about how the nation came to exist and to possess a land. The source material for what happened before the monarchy consisted of stories that had been passed down by oral tradition. Stories about legendary figures such as Abraham and Moses were no doubt told and retold for many years before anything was put into written form. While oral tradition can preserve accounts of events that actually occurred, we should keep in mind that stories passed on in this way can change over time in ways that reflect creative storytellers' efforts to speak meaningfully to new audiences and different circumstances.

Recall the account that introduces this chapter about an uncle's stories. To focus on how close his accounts are to what actually happened can mean missing much of what is going on when he tells a story. In the interest of being entertaining he may exaggerate or dramatize to help to make a point. We aren't deceived because we have some idea of what to expect. Similarly, when we take into account the purposes of biblical writers and the kind of source material they are using, we can avoid having unrealistic expectations about historical accuracy.

In some cases, we have reasons to think that a biblical story deviates significantly from what happened. Consider, for example, accounts of the conquest of Canaan. In the last chapter I questioned the truth of accounts that describe God as authorizing genocidal warfare. What may be surprising is that historical scholarship gives us reason to doubt the kind of wholesale extermination of Canaanites described in these accounts actually occurred.[7]

---

6. The idea that biblical narratives can serve theological purposes that affect how the story is told and what it includes applies to New Testament narratives too. Gospel writers can be recognized as having theological messages that they sometimes communicate in narrative form. For example, when Matthew describes the curtain of the Temple being torn from top to bottom (27:51) and saints rising from their tombs (27:52) in the aftermath of Jesus's crucifixion, it seems likely that he is making a theological point about the meaning of Jesus's death rather than recording historical events.

7. Enns, *Bible Tells Me So*, 58–60.

There are reasons both from the Bible itself and from sources external to biblical texts to question the depiction of events in the book of Joshua. For example, Jericho is one ancient site that has received extensive archeological study. This study does not support the account in Joshua of how the city was taken. Archeological evidence suggests that during the period in question there was only a minimal population in the area and no massive walls to fall down after trumpet blasts. For those who are not inclined to trust such evidence, there is also evidence about the conquest from the Bible itself. In Joshua we are told that particular groups were completely exterminated, but in biblical accounts of later events these groups are described as continuing to exist. It is as if the Bible itself is giving us clues that some descriptions of the conquest are not to be taken literally.

Acquaintance with literary genres from the ancient world gives us some indication of how we should read these descriptions. It appears that what we have in Joshua is a stylized account that resembles accounts from other Near Eastern nations that seek to glorify their conquests in a way that magnifies the nation's deity.[8] I mentioned previously that tribes from this period viewed national conquests as directly connected with the powers of the god who fought on behalf of the nation. So, in describing a relatively quick extermination of the nation's foes, what we apparently have is an Israelite version of praise for the powers of Yahweh. It may trouble us that the praise depends on exaggeration of Israel's military success. However, given that the account is written after Israel was well established in the land, we can imagine an ancient writer thinking the main point is that Yahweh gave the victory, even if there is embellishment in the details.

Potentially more problematic than the issue of the accuracy of the conquest narratives are questions about the accuracy of the biblical account of Israel's exodus from Egypt. There is a scholarly consensus that historical evidence does not support claims about an escape of slaves from Egypt as massive as the one described in the book of Exodus. The book describes over two million people (counting women and children) escaping, and it is hard to think that an event this huge would have left no historical traces. If we allow that the account is exaggerated, we can posit an event on a much smaller scale, but given that the story we have is based on oral traditions passed down over many years, it is difficult to say with confidence what the facts are.

What we can say is that the exodus event is described in biblical texts as a contest between Yahweh and the gods of Egypt.[9] The plague narrative

---

8. Wolterstorff, "Reading Joshua," 252–55.
9. Enns, *Bible Tells Me So*, 119–23.

is a not very subtle way of claiming that the gods of Egypt do not measure up to the God of Israel. For example, the Nile River was the heart of Egyptian life. Turning it to blood signifies the helplessness of the gods of Egypt against the power of Yahweh. The Egyptians represented one of their fertility gods as having the head of a frog. The second plague involves the land being overrun by frogs. The Sun god Ra was connected with Pharaoh's house, but in the ninth plague darkness covers the land. The final plague shows Yahweh's power over life and death as much greater than the power of the Egyptian god of the dead, Osiris. If we read these texts as a theological account intended to magnify the power of Yahweh, rather than a play-by-play description of historical events, we can view them as a narrative way of expressing the faith of Israel.

I want to guard against a possible misunderstanding. I am not saying that it is never important whether particular events described in the Bible actually occurred. I will be claiming later that the historical reality of some events is vital to Christian faith. But I am suggesting that robust Christian faith is compatible with recognizing that many biblical stories come to us in types of literature recognizably different from what we think of as historical reports. If we understand how this kind of literature was used in ancient contexts, we can avoid being troubled by misplaced expectations of historical accuracy.

It is helpful to view Israel's stories about events prior to life in the promised land as attempts to answer questions about national identity. Why do we worship Yahweh? How should we think about the practices that distinguish us from other people? What are Yahweh's purposes for the nation? The biblical response to such questions traces Jewish ancestry to the figure of Abraham who in response to encounters with God leaves his Mesopotamian homeland and receives promises about gaining a land, being the ancestor of a great nation, and participating in a divine blessing of the world. The narrative proceeds through multiple dramatic struggles punctuated by sibling rivalry on a massive scale and leading to slavery in the land of Egypt. We learn how Yahweh rescues the people from slavery, makes a covenant with the nation that includes instructions for how they are to conduct themselves, and brings them eventually to the land promised to their ancestor.

While I have suggested that we cannot know how much of this story to take as historical fact, we can recognize it as a satisfying way of thinking about the questions it addresses. The narrative provides a dramatic context in which the centrality of the community's faith in Yahweh makes sense. It is the kind of backstory that people can enter into imaginatively to think about who they are. Should we be troubled by questions about the historical accuracy of the account? That depends on how we think of God using these stories for purposes of revelation. Is God trying to communicate to us precise answers about what happened, or is God using these stories in a different way? If these stories in their ancient context were written to provide a kind of narrative explication of the faith of Israel, perhaps we should think of what we are offered here as a kind of window onto how that faith was understood. By entering into this narrative world, we can learn their way of thinking about who God is and what God is doing in the world.

One thing that becomes very clear is that in the stories biblical writers tell, they are describing a God who acts in our world of time and space. Their vision is different from that of a creator who stands aloof from the events of life. In these stories God has purposes and calls people to accomplish particular tasks. God's nature is revealed in what God does. These writers offer numerous interpretations of God's actions and plans. Some of their interpretations may seem defective in the light of fuller revelation, but they prepare us to consider our world as an arena for God's activity. When Jesus came proclaiming that God was establishing a new kind of kingdom, the people who heard him had been prepared to think in terms of God acting to achieve particular purposes in the world and expecting the fulfillment of what had been promised. When we enter into these stories, we are similarly prepared to consider our world in terms of what God has done, what God seeks to do now, and what God will do in the future.

CHAPTER 7

Revision within the Bible

A CENTRAL THEME OF this book is that a mature faith involves rethinking and revising religious claims in the light of new insights or new evidence. I don't mean to suggest that attempts to rethink the meaning of Christianity always result in an improvement. They can be seriously flawed. But I do mean to claim that the understanding of faith an individual starts with can be regarded as a version of the Christian message and that we sometimes have reason to judge particular versions of the faith to be defective. Such circumstances provide the occasion for trying to arrive at a better understanding than the one we have presumed.

While my focus has been on rethinking by individuals, revising our understanding of the Christian message is also a task for the Church as a whole. New knowledge and new cultural sensitivities have historically been an impetus for the Christian community to reformulate received teachings so that they continue to speak to people in contexts that differ from when they were originally formulated. What may not be obvious, however, is that this sort of readjustment and revision occurs within the Bible itself. In fact, understanding what is going on in some biblical texts involves recognizing that the author is taking issue with a teaching or a way of thinking found in other biblical texts.

The way churches taught me to think about the Bible was not conducive to recognizing when biblical authors were questioning what other biblical writers had said. Thinking of the Bible as a unitary message from God predisposed me to explain apparent differences away or sometimes not perceive them at all. Of course, as I matured, I could not help noticing significant differences of substance and style between different parts of the

Bible, but thinking of God as the real author inclined me to presume that while biblical authors might write from different perspectives, any apparent conflicts could be harmonized. Unfortunately, a disposition to smooth over the differences makes it much harder to give due attention to the claims of texts that say something genuinely new. It also hides from us how conflict between biblical authors can lead to revelatory advances.

Appreciating what is going on in the Bible means recognizing both continuity and discontinuity. Biblical writers work within the context of a developing tradition, even when they question aspects of that tradition. They don't disagree about everything. The kinds of disagreements they have typically presuppose agreement on many points. However, their differences sometimes indicate decision points for the direction the tradition will take. For example, we can find biblical texts that give nationalistic portrayals of God as on the side of Israel and indifferent or antagonistic toward other nations, but we also find universalistic portrayals of God's concern for all people. From a later perspective we can say that the universalistic understanding takes priority, but such a conclusion took time to reach. Reaching it meant viewing some ways of thinking that we find in biblical texts as needing to be significantly qualified or even rejected in the light of a fuller understanding.

Some people assume that rethinking anything in the Bible is off limits. However, biblical writers themselves do not make this assumption. They show a respect for the tradition they have inherited, but they do not assume the tradition is unalterable. Have you ever noticed that there are two versions of the ten commandments in the Bible that are not exactly the same? (Exod 20 and Deut 5). Surely if there is any document that Jews would think of as off limits to tampering because it is too sacred, the ten commandments should qualify. Yet what we find is a willingness to restate the commandments for a new time and a new situation. In fact, the book of Deuteronomy (which etymologically means "second law") is as a whole a rethinking of the requirements of law for a new generation.

RIGHTEOUSNESS AND WICKEDNESS

The book of Job is a good example of calling into question an understanding that is presupposed or explicitly stated in other biblical texts, namely that righteous living is rewarded and wickedness gets punished. This teaching is applied to the nation as a whole in the book of Deuteronomy and in historical accounts that the teaching in this book structures (Joshua through Second Kings). It is also applied to individuals throughout the book of

Proverbs and in some of the Psalms. For example, Ps 1 contrasts the life of the righteous individual with the life of the wicked person. The Psalmist says of the righteous, "In all that they do, they prosper" (1:3). On the other hand, "the wicked will not stand in the judgment" (1:5). So, good people have good lives, and bad people get their just deserts, at least in the long term. It is important to notice that these writers are not talking about rewards or punishments in the afterlife. Their claims about righteousness and wickedness are understood to apply to earthly fulfillments or punishments.

Given such a perspective, biblical writers frequently wrestle with the questions, "Why do the wicked prosper?" and "Why do the righteous suffer?" In some of the complaint Psalms these puzzles are offered to God almost as a kind of spur to provoke God to get on with the task of proper enforcement of the moral order. The book of Job questions the prevailing teaching on righteousness and wickedness by presenting us with the case of a righteous man who experiences undeserved suffering. Job's "comforters" accept a theology that holds Job's suffering can't really be undeserved and should be understood as a punishment for sin. They advise him to confess the sins that must have led to his plight. But Job insists, correctly according to the book, that he has done nothing to deserve the suffering that has come upon him.

The reader of the book of Job is told in the prologue that the explanation for Job's suffering has to do with events in the heavenly realm that the characters in the story know nothing about. It is problematic for us to read this account literally. The story of God taking a bet because of a challenge by "the adversary" portrays God in a way that seems deficient in relation to biblical teaching as a whole. However, we can treat the story as an imaginative way of conveying the idea that the explanation of human suffering often involves facts that humans are in no position to know.

People who accept the kind of theology the book of Job challenges recognize that what we observe often suggests that the righteous suffer unjustly and the wicked benefit from evil deeds. However, they insist that there must be a hidden justice that should lead us to deny what the appearances suggest. Taking this view for granted, Job's comforters cannot really consider the possibility that Job has done nothing to deserve the suffering he goes through. But the book of Job challenges their confident assumptions.

Who is right? Is it the prevailing theology that posits a strict correlation between righteousness and prosperity and wickedness and suffering, or is the critique we are offered in the book of Job correct? I think that the book of Job is correct in challenging ideas of a moral order that are overly simple. Perhaps we can say in general that doing what is right leads to a better life than being indifferent to right and wrong. But doing wrong can sometimes lead to desired outcomes, and doing right can sometimes lead to suffering. Furthermore, Jesus turns the traditional teaching on its head when he says that the blessed life the Psalmists talked about may well involve being persecuted and having people falsely say all sorts of horrible things against you (Matt 5:11). In fact, Jesus teaches that if you follow him, you need to be willing to accept the way of the cross. In other words, his followers are told to expect to suffer unjustly.

Of course, in Christian terms losing your life is described as a way to save it, but saving your life is clearly not equivalent to what we usually think of as earthly prosperity. Following Jesus can mean sacrificing things such as wealth or success or reputation or freedom because they seem less important than the value of knowing God and participating in God's work in the world. While we can call the way of life to which Jesus calls us genuine flourishing, we should not lose sight of the fact that this kind of flourishing is not what the Psalmists had in mind in speaking of the rewards of righteous living. Some people may want to speak here about heavenly rewards that are greater than whatever you lose. I will say more about such things in a subsequent chapter. But I will suggest here that we misunderstand the nature of heavenly rewards when we put them on a scale next to the kinds of earthly benefits the Psalmists had in mind. If these rewards are greater, it is from the perspective of people whose sense of value has shifted.

My main point here is that the Bible contains different messages about whether the righteous life is rewarded and the wicked life is punished. Job's message rejects an overly simple account that can also be found in the Bible, and the teaching of Jesus goes beyond Job in radically revising our understanding of what the good life is about.

ANIMAL SACRIFICE

Another example of biblical rethinking occurs in relation to the Jewish sacrificial system. It is difficult for most contemporary people to appreciate the centrality in Hebrew religion of killing animals and offering them as sacrifices to God. Our forms of worship are different. For us worship involves such activities as singing hymns and listening to sermons. We don't consider killing animals as a way to express our devotion to God. In fact, we may find the idea repulsive. However, the Jewish temple was built as a place to kill and offer animals as sacrifices. Animal sacrifices were not unique to the Hebrews. In the world where Jewish religion developed sacrifice was assumed to be the proper way to respond to a deity. Often this practice was conceived as a kind of bargain in which something is offered to a god and the god provides some benefit in return. The Hebrew Scriptures as a whole do not portray sacrifice in this way. But in multiple texts animal sacrifice is portrayed as something God requires.

Parts of Hebrew Scriptures go to great lengths to specify how sacrifices should be performed. The instructions are represented as coming directly from God. So, we might form the idea that God thinks offering sacrifices and doing so in precisely the right way is especially important. However, we also find numerous claims that suggest the importance of sacrifice needs to be rethought. In a passage that is quoted multiple times by Jesus, Hosea describes God as saying, "I desire steadfast love and not sacrifice, the knowledge of God rather than burnt offering" (Hos 6:6). Amos describes God as despising many kinds of religious practices, including acts of sacrifice, desiring instead acts of justice and righteousness (Amos 5:21–24). Ps 40 in a prayer to God includes the words, "Sacrifice and offering you do not desire ... Burnt offering and sin offering you have not required" (Ps 40:6). Instead of acts of sacrifice the Psalmist vows to do God's will.

What we have here, I think, is a reinterpretation of what God desires. Instead of thinking that worship of God is about performing the appropriate ritual acts in just the right way, an impression we could easily get from reading the book of Leviticus, these texts portray God as primarily concerned about righteous living, which includes acting from concern for the poor and oppressed. We don't have to read the prophets as rejecting the practice of sacrifice altogether. They might just be saying that when the practice is divorced from concern for justice and kindness, it loses its value. But such a claim is a shift away from thinking about ritual performance as achieving something by itself. It moves us in the direction of thinking that the value of these acts depends on whether or not they express genuine devotion to God.

I want to emphasize how significant this shift is. Once we start thinking of prescribed acts as ways to express gratitude and devotion to God, it is a short step to considering the possibility that the desired ends might be achieved in other ways. Eventually, when the Jewish temple is destroyed and temple worship is no longer possible, rabbinic authorities will rethink the importance of sacrifice. They will teach that prayer and acts of lovingkindness are appropriate substitutes for offering animal sacrifices.

This shift in Judaism resulted from adapting to a new situation when some biblical commands could no longer be followed literally. But the seeds for it were contained in the prophetic teaching that God cares more about righteous living than about animal sacrifices. In a later chapter I will claim that this shift has significant implications for how we should understand the death of Jesus. Here I am calling attention to the way the prophetic critique of traditional ways of thinking about sacrifice serves as a corrective to earlier views. To accept the idea that God is centrally concerned about whether we practice justice and mercy means thinking about religious observances differently.

CHRISTIAN REVISIONS

The New Testament itself is an example of a revision in how Jews who became Christians understood their sacred writings. Approaching these texts with a belief that God's purposes had been brought to fulfillment in a decisive way through Jesus was like finding a key that unlocked meanings they had not recognized before. As they reinterpreted what these texts said in the light of their new understanding of what God had done in Jesus, they had to rethink some of their fundamental assumptions.

In the churches of my youth, I was taught to think of many of the events described in the Gospels as fulfillments of biblical prophecy. By correlating prophetic texts with events in the life of Jesus, you were supposed to be able to see how what he did was anticipated, sometimes down to precise details. It might be imagined that this sort of correlation was what Jesus was calling attention to in a resurrection appearance when "beginning with Moses and all the prophets, he interpreted to them all the things about himself in all the scriptures" (Luke 24:27).

However, when you look at the New Testament texts that refer to scriptural prophecies, you are hard pressed to view many of these passages as predictions. For example, Matthew tells the story of how Mary and Joseph bring Jesus back from Egypt, where they had fled from Herod, and quotes a passage from Hos 11:1: "Out of Egypt I called my son." In the Hosea text, the son referred to is clearly the nation Israel, and the call is the rescue of the Jewish people from Egyptian slavery. So, it seems a stretch to think that what we have here is a prediction of an event in the life of Jesus.

However, we don't have to treat these texts as straightforward predictions to make sense of how New Testament writers applied them to Jesus. They saw a parallel between what God was doing with Israel and what God had done through the life of Jesus. That is, they thought of Jesus as fulfilling Israel's mission. So, it made sense to them to think that many of the things that had been said about the nation could be applied to Jesus. When they looked for this kind of parallel, they found it striking to think of Jesus, like the nation, as coming "out of Egypt."

Of course, there are some direct connections between what prophetic texts describe and events in the life of Jesus. But the clearest ones involve Jesus intentionally doing something with full awareness of what the prophetic text says. Although Jesus understood the mission of the Messiah differently from prevailing views of the time, he chose to act out the descriptions found in some Messianic texts. For example, his triumphal entry into Jerusalem was patterned on words from Isaiah and Zachariah. He was in effect announcing himself by these acts as the one these writings had anticipated. But for the most part, when New Testament writers see the story of Jesus as what the prophets were talking about, they are not picking out clear predictions with obvious fulfillments. They are instead rereading the ancient scriptural texts in the light of what they had come to see as the fulfillment of God's work in Jesus. They read with an understanding of how the story ends and use that understanding to find meanings that someone without this same understanding of the ending would not find.

What led them to read these scriptural texts with fresh eyes was a conviction that Jesus had actually risen from the dead. Without that conviction, Jesus would have been viewed as just another failed Messianic claimant. Nobody was expecting a crucified Messiah. Such an event didn't make sense within the context of Jewish thought, and resurrection was something that was expected only at the end of days. But being convinced that Jesus had risen from the dead assured them that Jesus actually had been sent by God, and this assurance meant that much of the received tradition had to be rethought. When Paul became convinced that he had come into contact with the risen Christ, it took him a period of extended study and reflection by himself in Arabia to reformulate his understanding of what God was doing (Gal 1:17).

An important part of Paul's rethinking dealt with the significance of the Jewish Law (Torah). As a trained rabbi, he presumed the centrality of the Torah in God's plans. As any pious Jew would affirm, what God wanted most was obedience to the Torah's requirements. But Paul's conviction that he had encountered a crucified and risen Messiah led him to change his mind about much of what he thought he understood. God's purposes, he concluded, were not really centered on keeping the commandments found in the Torah.[1] In Galatians he compares the Law to a childhood tutor serving the temporary purpose of preparing the way until God's full purposes can be revealed in the Messiah (Gal 3:24). It is through Jesus, Paul says, not through the Torah, that the powers of sin and death have been defeated.

It is not just Paul who seeks to rethink the meaning of the Hebrew Scriptures in the light of Jesus. All the New Testament writers do so. For example, the book of Hebrews (which was not written by Paul) portrays Jesus as a high priest who fulfills the sacrificial system in such a way that

---

1. Enns, *Bible Tells Me So*, 219–23.

there is no more need for sacrifices. Other New Testament texts offer different ways of understanding what Jesus had accomplished, but all of them revise traditional ways of understanding Scripture in the light of what God has done through the Messiah.

New Testament texts have a unique kind of authority for Christians because they were written by the primary witnesses to God's revelation in Christ. Later writers may formulate and communicate important Christian truths, but the testimony of those who lived during or shortly after the events that gave birth to the church is foundational for whatever Christian reflection follows. Nevertheless, we cannot just repeat what those texts say and dispense with further thinking. Like the biblical writers, we have to rethink received teaching in ways that make sense for us. If we think that God guided the process that led to their accounts, we should be able to think that God is still involved in the process by which we seek to understand what has been revealed.

CHAPTER 8

Ethics and Culture

SUPPOSE THAT YOU ARE reading the Bible and come across the following passage from Deuteronomy:

> If someone has a stubborn and rebellious son who does not obey his father and mother, who does not heed them when they discipline him, then his father and mother shall take hold of him and bring him out to the elders of his town at the gate of that place. They shall say to the elders of his town, "This son of ours is stubborn and rebellious. He will not obey us. He is a glutton and a drunkard." Then all the men of the town shall stone him to death (Deut 21:18–21).

The problem dealt with in this text is recognizable. You may know people who have struggled with defiant children who seem bent on sabotaging their lives; you may even have clashed with intractable children of your own. However, the proposed solution comes as a shock. Even if you are a parent who has major difficulties with your children, I doubt that you will think that the procedure described here is a viable solution to your problem. Public execution of self-willed children is not an option you would consider. But why not? The instruction is right there in the scriptural text. So, if you believe in doing what the Bible says to do, how can you refuse to accept this teaching?

The answer can't just be you think that following this instruction will run afoul of the law. Even if you are confident you could escape prosecution, my guess is that you think there is something wrong with inflicting capital punishment on rebellious children. If you heard one of your neighbors proposing it, you would likely be morally outraged. But again, it's right there in the Bible, so how can you question instructions from God?

Perhaps you could claim that the instructions do not really apply to you or your contemporaries, but are God's commands for how ancient Israelites should handle this type of situation. No doubt you do make a similar distinction with regard to some instructions in Hebrew Scriptures, such as the food laws. God may have told Israelites not to eat pork or shrimp, but those commands, you might say, are not for all people at all times. They are addressed to a particular group, and perhaps they are for a limited time period.

But while you might make such a distinction with regard to some biblical commands, the teaching about executing recalcitrant children does not look like the kind of instruction that you can easily think of as revealing how God wants anyone to behave. People of the time may have believed this conduct was divinely authorized, but we can't help asking whether a completely good and wise God couldn't have come up with something better. To say the least, the directive does not strike us as morally advanced.

Nor is this command the only one in Hebrew Scriptures that seems questionable on moral grounds. Consider an incident from Num 15:

> When the Israelites were in the wilderness, they found a man gathering sticks on the sabbath day. Those who found him gathering sticks brought him to Moses, Aaron, and to the whole congregation. They put him in custody because it was not clear what should be done to him. Then the Lord said to Moses, "The man shall be put to death; all the congregation shall stone him outside the camp." The whole congregation brought him outside the camp and stoned him to death, just as the Lord had commanded Moses (Num 15:32–36).

We can recognize the way of thinking that prescribes executing a man who gathers sticks in violation of sabbath rules as similar to views we have encountered in our own time. We sometimes hear people say, "Rules are rules," and often these people imagine God as operating from the same kind of inflexible mindset. But most of us think that some discernment about applying rules and invoking punishments is needed, especially when we are talking about an extreme punishment for what looks to us like a relatively minor violation. Even if we think that some kind of strictness is needed to ensure the rules are generally followed, we would likely regard the death penalty in a case of this sort as inordinate. Saying this instruction was only for a particular group of people during a limited time period doesn't help much because it is hard to think that the kind of God Jesus talked about would issue such a command.

So far, I have given only two examples from Hebrew Scriptures of acts punishable by death. However, the list of crimes for which the death penalty is prescribed is much wider. The specified offenses include a woman who is found not to be a virgin on her wedding night (Deut 22:20–21), adultery (Deut 22:22), and sex between a man and a woman betrothed to someone else (Deut 22:23). Sexual acts between two men (Lev 20:13) or sexual acts with animals (Lev 20:15) are also listed as punishable by death. Other acts subject to the death penalty include cursing a parent (Lev 20:9), blasphemy (Lev 24:16), and enticing people to worship other gods (Deut 13:6–10).

Even if you think that the death penalty is appropriate under some circumstances, you may find it alarming how widely it is applied. While we can agree that adultery is morally wrong, hardly anyone in our time thinks we should punish this wrong by execution. And what about blasphemy? We may find it grossly offensive, but do we need to kill the perpetrator? There are still countries today with laws against blasphemy that prescribe the death penalty, but most of us find such laws a throwback to a less civilized era. We find it unpersuasive when defenders of these laws try to justify them by referring to commands found in sacred texts.

The point here is that some instructions in Hebrew Scripture seem to us morally deficient. If we think of them as products of an era in which people operated under different assumptions that colored their thinking about right and wrong, we can comprehend why such teachings might have been accepted. We may even in some cases be able to reconstruct a rationale that explains why particular instructions might have seemed proper to people of the time. For example, if we presume the widespread ancient view that parental authority is analogous to divine authority, we can see why persistent willful disobedience to parents might have been regarded as a major sacrilege that in extreme cases deserves death. But we no longer think in ways that make these practices seem justifiable, and when we consider them in the light of the revelation of God in Jesus, they don't seem to measure up. Can you imagine Jesus endorsing execution of a rebellious child or handling a case of Sabbath violation by advocating public execution?

Of course, biblical authors who wrote these instructions understandably regarded the legal code they lived by to have divine authority. We wouldn't expect them to make subtle distinctions that come from a later era about how human understanding of what God authorizes can be shaped by culturally situated views of right and wrong. But we should not avoid making such distinctions ourselves. Just as we acknowledge that these writers presume the scientific views of their time in describing creation, we should acknowledge that they think and write in terms of the moral frameworks of their time in describing what God expects of them. If we are using these texts for our own guidance, we have to filter out claims shaped by culture that we have reason to judge morally deficient.

It might be thought that I am denying divine revelation. I am not. But I am claiming that revelation does not work through overriding human thought processes. Whatever God reveals comes through human understanding that is subject to the limits that go with making assumptions that seem obvious to people who inhabit a particular culture during a particular time period. What biblical writers claim about right and wrong is communicated in a form that fits with their ways of thinking, and we judge some of their ways of thinking to be products of the time that we cannot attribute to God. Of course, we have to admit that our own understanding is also limited by the culture we inhabit. But we can recognize our fallibility while also affirming that the revelatory process has made some truths abundantly clear.

One of the consequences of acknowledging a significant human element in revelation is that some common ways of supporting particular moral views by citing what a biblical text condemns or permits should be recognized as overly simple. We have to ask not only what a text says, but also whether the cultural assumptions that underlie what it says are consistent with ethical teaching of the fuller biblical tradition. Practices that may have seemed unobjectionable, given the thinking of the era, can be rejected in the light of the realization that they are inconsistent with loving your neighbor as yourself or some other deep revelatory truth about God's purposes for human life.

SLAVERY

The danger of misreading ethical teaching from the Bible by failing to take into account the way it can be bound up with cultural assumptions of the period can be highlighted by noticing how Christians have used the Bible to claim that slavery is a permissible institution. If there is any ethical truth that seems clear and obvious to us now, it is that slavery is wrong. When we look at biblical texts, we are not in danger of thinking that we should conclude that the practice is permissible. But when our ancestors looked at the same Bible, they often reached different conclusions.

Notice first that there is no specific condemnation of slavery in the Bible. In the Jewish Law we do get regulations about how the institution should be practiced, but no suggestion that there is anything unacceptable about owning other people, as long as the regulations are followed. That some people are property was taken as an obvious fact in the world biblical writers inhabited. Among ancient Near Eastern societies of the time, an individual could become a slave in various ways. Some became slaves by being captured in war. Some were purchased from other nations. Defaulting on a debt could result in slavery. Children could be sold by their parents as slaves during times of economic distress. People in dire economic conditions could even sell themselves as slaves.[1]

Regulations for the institution of slavery are given in Exod 21, Deut 15, and Lev 25. The rules in Exodus say that slaves who are Hebrew males must be released after six years. Exodus lists as an exception a situation where the man is married during the period of slavery and may choose to remain with his wife and children by becoming a slave for life (Exod 21:2–6). In the Exodus account, a female Hebrew slave who was sold by her father does not have the right to leave after six years. She can be released only if the master no longer wants her as a concubine for himself or a son (Exod 21:7–11).

By contrast the rules in Deuteronomy say that both male and female Hebrew slaves have to be set free after six years. This text also specifies that they are to be given provisions when set free. In Leviticus there are additional restrictions about treatment of Hebrew slaves. We are told that Hebrews who have entered into servitude because of debt are to be treated as hired workers rather than slaves (Lev 25:39–43). The text also specifies that they are not to be treated harshly. On the other hand, the period of servitude allowed in Leviticus is potentially longer than the six years described in Exodus or Deuteronomy, since the date of release is specified as the next year of Jubilee, which would occur only in fifty-year intervals.

One thing to notice in these texts is that the rules are explicitly about how to treat Hebrew slaves. They don't apply to non-Israelites. So, we may presume that harsh treatment of foreign slaves is permitted. Furthermore, some texts that give us an idea of the sort of harsh treatment that might occur don't really distinguish between Hebrew and non-Hebrew. Consider the following teaching from Exodus: "When a slaveowner strikes a male or female slave with a rod and the slave dies immediately, the owner shall be punished. But if the slave survives a day or two, there is no punishment; for the slave is the owner's property" (Exod 21:20–21).

The assumption here is that beating slaves, and presumably other harsh treatment, is to be expected. They are after all, according to the text, the owner's property. To be sure, if an owner is so violent that immediate death occurs, there will be some penalty, but we should suspect that

1. Mendelsohn, "Slavery in the OT," 384–85.

the punishment will be relatively minor. There won't be a question of being charged with the equivalent of murder or manslaughter.

In these texts the practice of some human beings taking other human beings as property is treated as normal. There is no indication that there is anything objectionable about owning slaves or selling them, even if there are some restrictions that govern how fellow Israelites are to be treated. It might be imagined that by the time we get to the New Testament, everything has changed, but it has not. New Testament texts also presume that some people are masters and others slaves. Slaves are instructed to accept their lot in life and obey their masters (e.g., Eph 5: 5-8). While Christian slaveowners are instructed not to abuse their slaves and even to treat them with kindness, there is no teaching that they should stop being slaveowners or that they should work toward ending of the institution of slavery.

So perhaps it is understandable that many of our ancestors took it for granted that slavery was a divinely authorized practice. When opposition to slavery arose in the nineteenth century, defenders of the practice included some prominent Christian theologians. Some of them distinguished between slavery itself and unjust characteristics of the way it is practiced at particular times and places.[2] So, for example, they claimed that owning slaves is not wrong in itself, but it is wrong to treat slaves unjustly by keeping them uneducated or giving them no marital and parental rights. In other words, there is no problem with making some people property if there are appropriate limits to the owner's use of the property.

In arguments of the time defenders of slavery could appeal to a great many specific biblical texts to support slavery, whereas opponents tended to focus on a few general scriptural principles. Kenton Sparks cites the example of John Wesley, whose anti-slavery writings inspired other abolitionists of the time. He says,

> What is interesting about Wesley's rhetoric is that his written deliberations on slavery hardly use Scripture at all. He mainly describes the gross cruelties of slavery and takes the evil of the institution as self-evident. . . . He has ignored those texts that seem to legitimize slavery and trumped them with texts that call upon Christians to love their fellows and to treat them with dignity and respect . . .[3]

When we look at Scripture today, we can find various general principles that seem to us to undermine slavery. For example, Paul writes, "There is no longer Jew nor Greek, there is no longer slave nor free, there is no

2. Sparks, *God's Word in Human Words*, 290.
3. Sparks, *God's Word in Human* Words, 291.

longer male and female, for all of you are one in Christ Jesus" (Gal 3:28). Paul saw the Christian message as breaking down many of the cultural barriers that divided people, but even so, he did not spell out the conclusion that slavery is wrong. He did advise a particular slaveowner to take back a runaway slave "no longer as a slave but more than a slave, a beloved brother" (Phlm 16). But he does not say that all slaves should be released. It is only after many centuries that Christians attain unity in understanding that there is something fundamentally inconsistent between Christian teachings and the practice of slavery.

The point here is that scriptural teachings about right and wrong often presuppose standard cultural practice. But many of the practices that are taken for granted in these texts can be judged inconsistent with fundamental teachings of the faith, even if it takes a long time to recognize their inconsistency. We can now see clearly that owning another person as property does not fit with loving your neighbor as yourself or treating others as we want to be treated, but to say that biblical teaching opposes slavery, we have to overrule scriptural texts in which slavery is treated as an acceptable practice.

WOMEN

Here is a biblical passage that you ought to find startling: "If a man meets a virgin who is not engaged, and seizes her and lies with her . . . the man who lay with her shall give fifty shekels of silver to the young woman's father, and she shall become his wife" (Deut 22:28–29). Let me rephrase that: Someone who rapes an unmarried and unengaged woman has to marry her and make a monetary payment to her father. There are several things to notice here. One is that there is no mention of the woman having any choice. She has to marry the man who assaulted her. A passage in Exod 22 that may cover this case says that the father can refuse to give her in marriage, but still gets the bride-price. So, whether she marries the rapist is apparently the father's choice. But why does the father get paid? Apparently, the unmarried girl is regarded as belonging to him, and he gets protection for the loss of value caused by the rape. The whole focus is on harm to the father and not on the harm to the attacked woman.

It is hard for us to wrap our heads around this sort of rule. We have to imagine a world where a daughter's status is thought of on the model of property. The father decides when and if she gets married, and he is entitled to monetary compensation when her economic value is lessened. Nor is this way of thinking limited to unmarried women. Recall one of the ten commandments. In Exod 20:17 we are told: "You shall not covet your neighbor's house; you shall not covet your neighbor's wife, or male or female slave, or ox or donkey, or anything that belongs to your neighbor." Notice that the wife is listed along with other property that one might covet, including the house and slaves.

I don't mean to suggest that in these times women were treated only as property. But it seems clear that women were regarded as under the authority of men. The daughter would be under the father's control initially and later under the control of the man her father accepted as her husband. Note also that a woman could not choose to end a marriage. There were provisions in Jewish law for a man to divorce a woman who displeased him, but no provisions for a woman to initiate divorce.

In New Testament texts, written many years later, the authority of men over women is assumed. Biblical authors repeat a standard instruction in the Greco-Roman world: that women are to "be subject" to their husbands (e.g., Col 3:18). We do get additional teachings that seem to soften the presumption of male control. Husbands are told to love their wives and not to treat them harshly (Col 3:18). In Ephesians Christian husbands are told that they should love their wives "as Christ loved the church and gave himself up for her" (Eph 5:25). Also framing the Ephesian discussion of duties is the intriguing idea of submission to each other (Eph 5:21). But while these teachings are potentially transformative, they leave in place fundamental societal assumptions about the place of women.

One thing that seems clear is that women in the early church were experiencing a degree of freedom from the limits of some role expectations. In the context of church meetings, they were doing things that women generally didn't do in public. In some New Testament texts, the concern seems to be that women not disregard standard social norms to the extent that they bring disrepute on the community. So, for example, women are told to wear a veil over their heads when they pray or prophesy in worship (1 Cor 11:2–3).

Most contemporary Christians understand instructions about such things as wearing veils or the length of hair or greeting others with a holy kiss as expressions of cultural norms that don't apply universally. However, many Christians accept as universally applicable teachings such as, "Let a woman learn in silence with full submission. I permit no woman to teach or have authority over a man, she is to keep silent . . . she will be saved through childbearing . . . " (1 Tim 2:11–15). Note, however, the justification given in this text. The reason women should not teach is that Eve was deceived, not Adam. Apparently, the author (which most scholars take not to be Paul) finds women gullible in a way that men are not. This claim sounds to me like a theological rationalization of a preexisting cultural prejudice. If we are willing to admit that scriptural teachings about slaves can display moral blind-spots, shouldn't we also be alert to the possibility that particular biblical teachings about women's place may be shaped by culturally conditioned views of female roles that a deep understanding of the Christian message gives us reason to judge deficient?

SAME-SEX SEXUALITY

Many Christians find homosexual acts unacceptable on the basis of scriptural teaching. They point to particular texts in which they find unequivocal declarations that such behavior is wrong, and perhaps not merely wrong, but especially despicable. They can't see how anyone who accepts biblical authority could think otherwise. But as I hope this chapter makes clear, it often takes careful thinking to determine how particular biblical prohibitions and permissions are applicable to our judgments about right and wrong.

Given the importance some Christians assign to condemning homosexual acts, it may be surprising that there are only a few passages in the Bible that address this topic. Eight texts are commonly quoted, and it is not even clear that all those texts are relevant. For example, the wrong described in the story of Sodom and Gomorrah looks more like gang rape than any kind of voluntary sexual activity. You can find a more straightforward condemnation of sexual acts between two males in Lev 18:22 and 20:13. Both texts refer to the prohibited act as a male lying "with a male as with a woman" and call doing so an abomination. Before we declare the matter settled, however, we should notice that hardly anyone wants to say that all the prohibitions of Leviticus apply to us. Forbidden acts include such things as wearing a garment made of different materials (Lev 19:19), having a tattoo (Lev 19:28), eating shrimp or other unclean foods (Lev 11), planting different kinds of seeds in the same field (Lev 19:19), and having sex with a woman during her menstrual period (Lev 18:19). If we think that homosexual acts are unacceptable because Leviticus says so, we need to be able to explain why this prohibition should be applied to us while others should not.

The practices called abominations in Leviticus and other places in Hebrew Scripture include some things that seem puzzling to us when we try to think of them as moral prohibitions. The most common word translated as abomination (*toevah*) refers to things that are thought of as abhorrent to God. A central application of the term is to idolatrous practices. Maintaining purity means keeping clear of participating in the worship of other gods. But eating unclean food is also described as an abomination (Lev 20:25), as is wearing clothes of the opposite sex (Deut 22:5). In other words, the term is applied to a wide range of forbidden practices that includes some acts that don't strike most of us as moral violations.

Some of the acts condemned in Leviticus involve blurring the lines between different types of things. For example, breeding different types of animals or planting different kinds of seeds together or wearing a garment made of different materials (Lev 19:19). Very likely there is a similar concern behind the command not to wear clothes of the other gender. That is, males should behave like males and females like females; anything that blurs the line is unholy or unclean. The way the prohibition of sexual acts between males is stated suggests that this prohibition is also connected with concern about gender roles. Men should not act sexually toward other men in a way that involves one playing the female role. Some scholars have thought that the revulsion that such acts may have evoked is connected with the view that it is demeaning for a man to assume a role thought beneath him.[4] Regardless of whether these scholars are correct, we seem to be dealing with judgments based on what is regarded as normal or abnormal, given the understanding of gender roles of the time. When the culturally shaped assumptions about male and female roles are removed, it is unclear what basis there is for thinking of the prohibitions as universally applicable.

Paul's comments in Rom 1, like the Leviticus text, are often thought to be decisive in establishing the impermissibility of same-sex erotic acts. He speaks disdainfully of women "exchanging natural intercourse for unnatural" and "men giving up natural intercourse with women to commit shameless acts with men" (Rom 1:26–7). It is not surprising that someone trained in Jewish rabbinic tradition would presume the kind of negative view of homosexual acts found in Leviticus. However, Paul's account suggests reasons that go beyond the category of uncleanness that underlies the prohibitions in the ancient holiness code. He characterizes the activities he describes as involving excessive passion, and he uses terms such as "degrading," "shameless," and "unnatural."

In considering what Paul says, it is important to understand how acts of this type were conceived in the ancient world. Scholars agree that ancient people did not have our concept of sexual orientation. When we think of homosexual acts, we mostly imagine people whose sexual desire is predominantly or exclusively directed toward members of the same sex. We also recognize on the basis of empirical evidence that for the most part, those

---

4. In ancient cultures, including Hebrew culture, there was a strong sense that men being treated as females was especially degrading or shameful. The terrible stories of Gen 19 and Judg 19 in which females are offered to rapists as substitutes for men might be interpreted as showing that male rape was regarded in this culture as a more heinous offence than female rape because the degradation to men was viewed as so repugnant.

who have such desires are not able to change them. However, writers in Paul's time thought of people who engaged in these acts as having ordinary heterosexual desires, but seeking out additional kinds of sexual pleasure as well. James Brownson describes their way of conceiving things as follows:

> as we can see from a variety of ancient sources contemporaneous with Paul, same-sex eroticism was consistently portrayed by those who opposed this behavior as a manifestation of a form of insatiable lust that, not content with heterosexual relations, was driven to increasingly exotic and perverse forms of sexual behavior that had become grotesque through ever expanding self-indulgence.[5]

Paul's description of people "exchanging natural intercourse for unnatural" and being "consumed with passion for one another" seems to fit this way of conceiving homosexual acts.

Furthermore, the most prominent examples of this kind of activity in the culture of the time were acts initiated by those with greater status or power who could enforce their will on someone. The paradigm cases involved a master and a slave, an older man and a young boy, and sex involving prostitutes.[6] If cases of this sort are Paul's focus, it is easy to see why he might react to a man engaged in such activities with disgust. Indeed, some commentators think Paul's description is a veiled reference to the well-known excesses of Roman emperors, such as Caligula. While we can agree with Paul in condemning such excesses, there is ample reason to think he was not imagining the kind of long-term committed same-sex relationship defended by some Christians today.

In addition to the characterization of the acts he condemns as involving a kind of out-of-control passion, Paul also speaks of them as shameless and unnatural. When writers in the time of Paul use the terms "unnatural" and "shameless" in relation to same-sex erotic acts, they tend to be thinking about violations of established gender roles. Men, it was thought, were the dominant and active partner, whereas women had a passive role. In same-sex acts the roles were confused, and in societies that thought of women as inferior, participation in the confusion of roles was often judged to be degrading or disgraceful for men. It is noteworthy that Paul uses the same terms that appear in Rom 1 (natural, unnatural, and degrading) to talk about men having short hair and women having long hair (1 Cor 11:13–15). So, we have some cause to wonder whether the judgments in Rom 1 about what is natural or degrading that have been taken as a basis for a blanket

---

5. Brownson, *Bible, Gender, Sexuality*, 166.
6. Vines, *God and the Gay Christian*, 104.

condemnation of all homosexual acts depend on what we would call social conventions of the time.

I don't mean to suggest that the behaviors Paul has in mind don't involve a despicable moral depravity. But it seems clear is that what Paul was condemning is not the same as what contemporary Christians who argue that homosexual acts can be permissible are defending. It is a stretch to take his words to apply to a committed relationship of a same-sex couple. Such a possibility was not on his radar. To consider it, he would have needed to think in terms of our concept of sexual orientation that is not a matter of choice and then applied Christian principles to how someone with such an orientation should live. We have to work out for ourselves some of what he could not realistically have considered.

In this chapter I have been showing how using the Bible to reach ethical conclusions often requires us to recognize that biblical authors wrote from cultural perspectives that we have reason to question. If we believe in progressive revelation, we can think that within the Bible less adequate understandings are often corrected by more adequate ones. But in cases such as the role of women or same-sex behavior, the process of reflection may need to continue well beyond any conclusion we can draw from biblical texts alone. We inhabit a different world in which we may acquire reasons for questioning some ancient assumptions and have experiences that lead us to rethink some traditional ideas.

One kind of experience that has been an impetus for many Christians in rethinking their views on same-sex relationships is encountering people who through of no choice of their own feel sexual desires toward members of their own gender. Biblical scholar James Brownson reports how he revised his stance on the issue of homosexuality and wrote a book explaining why after his eighteen-year-old son revealed his sexual orientation. Brownson confesses that after considering the issue in relation to someone he knew well, he found traditional treatments, including his own prior thinking, shallow and unhelpful.[7] For him, being faithful to biblical revelation meant changing his mind about how the relevant biblical texts should be understood and how they should be applied in the contemporary context.

---

7. Brownson, *Bible, Gender, Sexuality*, 11–12.

PART 3

Rethinking Christian Teaching

CHAPTER 9

What Does the Death of Jesus Mean?

IN THE CHURCHES I attended growing up, the explanation I was given of the meaning of the death of Jesus went something like this:

> All human beings deserve the punishment of hell for their sins, and the justice of God requires that such punishment be given. But Jesus has taken our place and endured the punishment we deserve. His sacrifice has appeased God's wrath against us so that we can receive forgiveness, if only we accept what Jesus has done on our behalf.

I didn't know it at the time, but the teaching I received was a version of what is called the penal substitutionary theory of the atonement. Protestant Reformers, such as John Calvin, offered the theory as an explanation of biblical teaching about what the death of Jesus accomplished. This theory is usually considered to be a variant of an earlier substitution view: the satisfaction theory of the atonement developed by Anselm in the eleventh century. Writing in a medieval context where breaches of honor and demands for satisfaction were an important part of social life, Anselm proposed that human sin was an affront to God's honor and that the death of Jesus provided the kind of satisfaction needed to preserve that honor. Anselm said that we couldn't provide the needed satisfaction ourselves, but Jesus did it on our behalf.

Throughout the history of the church there have been various proposals about how to explain the significance of Jesus's death, but no real consensus that a particular account is the uniquely correct way of understanding its meaning. Nevertheless, churches like the ones I attended presented the penal substitutionary theory as *the Christian teaching* on why Jesus died. I was taught nothing about alternative accounts or the historical origins of this view or the range of theological discussion on the topic. I don't think that my teachers knew about such matters. As a child, I was not in a good position to assess what my elders presented to me as authoritative truth. But as I grew older, I came to think that the version of Christian teaching I had received was seriously flawed.

One reason for questioning the penal substitutionary theory is that it seems to portray the Father and the Son as having divergent attitudes that appear to be in tension with each other. The Father is wrathful and needs to be appeased, while the Son displays sacrificial love for sinners. The account suggests a rule-bound Father who is ready to inflict punishment in contrast with a Son who goes out of his way to rescue us. Perhaps, however, this characterization is misleading. After all, the Father is described in some biblical passages as sending the Son on his mission. So perhaps the Father is eager to forgive, but somehow bound by the requirements of justice. However, it is hard to make sense of the idea that God is bound in this way. There is no difficulty in thinking that God takes sin seriously and views it as a blight on creation, but thinking that God is compelled to demand that sinners receive harsh punishment suggests a deity very different from the father in a famous parable of Jesus who displays extravagant and unexpected love and forgiveness toward the one we call the prodigal son. With that father, it is not the need for just punishment that seems preeminent, but a willingness to cast dignity aside and offer mercy and love to bring about a restored relationship.

The penal substitutionary theory portrays the death of Jesus as a way to shift the Father's attitude from wrath to love. Even if we can make sense of the claim that some kind of shift in attitude is needed in order for the Father to forgive, does it make sense to think that the death of Jesus could produce this kind of shift? If the problem is that God requires just punishment, how can the death of an innocent person appease righteous wrath against those who deserve punishment? We may be able to think of stories in which one person voluntarily accepts the punishment that someone else deserves. I have heard such stories in sermons. But if God's justice means giving people what they deserve, no amount of suffering by someone innocent results in justice being done. How is it exactly that we are imagining God when we think that God is able to excuse the guilty because someone innocent suffers? Do we imagine that God demands blood be shed and that it doesn't matter whether the one whose blood is shed is the guilty party or not? That picture sounds more like a pagan deity than a God motivated by love.

I think the idea that the death of Jesus is needed to appease God's wrath puts us on the wrong track. In the penal substitutionary theory God's wrath is understood as a manifestation of a concern to give proper punishment to wrongdoers. If we view God's concern for justice as a kind of impersonal enforcement of the moral order, then it seems to be in tension with God's love. But suppose we reject the idea that there is such a conflict of motivations within God and think of God's concern for justice as an expression of God's love. To do so, we need an alternative way to understand God's concern for justice.

We can find such an alternative in the Bible. An important biblical theme is that God seeks to bring healing and restoration to the world. What God seeks has been called restorative justice in contrast to punitive or retributive justice, which is focused on punishing the guilty.[1] It is a concern to make people righteous rather than making sure that they suffer enough for their misdeeds. Thinking of God's justice in this way removes the need to posit that a certain amount of suffering is needed so that God can forgive us. What is needed is a removal of the barriers we may erect to God's work of restoration.

Rather than thinking that the cross enables God to shift from attitudes of wrath to attitudes of love, we might instead think that it has more to do with shifting our attitudes. If the problem is our resistance to God's intentions, we might be willing to drop our resistance if we could see vividly the lengths to which God is willing to go to bring us restoration and healing. In other words, the cross of Jesus might be a revelation of God's love with the power to motivate us to lay down our resistance.

But that idea is not quite enough to explain the meaning of the death of Jesus. My willingness to die for someone may show how much I care about that person. But if my death is not a result of something that I am doing for the other individual, it is not really a revelation of love. So even if we say that what is needed is not a change in God's attitude, but in ours, an explanation of the death of Jesus calls for some account of how his death is a consequence of something God is doing for us.

HE DIED FOR US

In 1 Corinthians 15 Paul quotes what appears to be an early Christian confession of faith. He cites this confession in the context of discussing the resurrection of Jesus. But it contains the following affirmation about his death: "Christ died for our sins." The penal substitutionary theory is one way of

---

1. Flood, *Healing the Gospel*, 9–16.

understanding this affirmation. It interprets the claim to mean that Jesus suffered the punishment that we deserve so that we could be pardoned. However, a different way to think about what Christ did is to view it not as a transaction that somehow balances the books, but as a consequence of a costly rescue mission. We are familiar with cases in which human rescuers do something to save another person even at the risk of their own injury or death. In such cases the injury or death of the rescuer is not the goal, but might be a consequence of performing the rescue. Saying that Christ died for our sins could be a way of saying that God in Christ does what it takes to rescue us from sin and that a consequence of this action is Jesus's suffering and death.

The idea of being rescued from sin can seem odd if we think of sin primarily as a matter of rule violations that should be either punished or excused. But at its root, sin is more fundamentally a distortion of human concerns that keeps us from achieving our true calling and puts us on paths that are destructive, both individually and socially. Inordinate desires for such things as money or sex or prestige or control can exert a power over us that makes us captives. Being rescued would mean being set free from what holds us captive so that we can live the kind of life God intends for us. But how can God's action in Jesus set us free?

First, I think it is a mistake to focus exclusively on Jesus's death in isolation from his life. I have heard preachers say Jesus was born to die, as if that was the only important thing he did. Surely, there is something strange about that way of thinking. It seems to dismiss Jesus's actions and his teachings as mere preliminaries to the main event. We need to shift our focus. The central thing God does in Jesus is what Christians call the incarnation, a union between God and humanity that is displayed in the whole of Jesus's life, not just the events of the last week. Those climatic events are part of a larger story of how God identifies with the human plight enough to share it with us. That identification ultimately leads to death, but to understand the significance of Jesus's death, we need to place it within the context of the larger story.

Second, focusing on God's overall project suggests a way Jesus's life and death might deal with human sin. We can think of God's identification with human life as fulfilling a previously unrealized human potential. Jesus shows us a human life that is fully dedicated to God. He lives a life that is freed from the idolatrous concerns that hold us captive. If this new way of being human could be shared with us, we might acquire the freedom we need. New Testament teachings point toward this kind of sharing. For example, as he faced death, Jesus invited his followers to share in his body and blood. Receiving holy communion can be understood as a symbolic exhibition of our willingness to receive the kind of life he offers us. New Testament authors describe in various ways what it means to participate in this new life through the work of God's Spirit.

According to the penal substitutionary theory, the cross is a means of getting the penalty of sin paid so that God can offer forgiveness. In the alternative I am describing the cross is a consequence of what God does to free us from the power of sin. But why is it a consequence? The answer, I think, is that for Jesus living a life wholly dedicated to God meant faithfulness to a mission to serve as a human representative of God in the world. The cross was a consequence of Jesus's doing what he was called to do. The gospel stories portray him as predicting that what he was doing would lead to his suffering and death. It is not that he was seeking suffering and death. Instead, he was seeking to maintain his path, even while recognizing that doing so would lead to crucifixion.

JESUS'S MISSION AND THE CROSS

It wouldn't have taken superhuman knowledge for Jesus to recognize that he was arousing opposition from Jewish leaders and that they were likely to do everything in their power to stop him from disrupting things. In fact, Jesus intentionally did some things that he knew were likely to produce opposition. For example, he went into the Jewish temple and drove out the money-changers. This action was an in-your-face challenge to the Jewish religious system that provoked the religious leaders to do what they could to get rid of this troublesome upstart. From their point of view, he was messing up a divinely ordained order.

Jesus was in fact challenging the established order. In a variety of symbolic actions and direct teachings he proclaimed a God who had higher priorities than Sabbath observance and ritual purity. In the tradition of Old Testament prophets Jesus quoted Hosea's message that God wants mercy rather than sacrifice, and he exhibited God's priorities in his ministry to the poor and oppressed. The kind of God Jesus proclaimed was one whose expansive love welcomed the outcasts and challenged the self-righteous who lacked concern for those they deemed beneath them.

In one of his parables Jesus portrayed God as a landowner who sends multiple messengers to get the tenants who were occupying the land to pay what they owe. The tenants abuse the various messengers in ways that echo how the Jewish people had treated prophetic messengers in the past. Finally, as a last resort the landowner sends his son to make an appeal, and the tenants see this event as the opportunity to kill the heir and take the land for themselves (Matt 21:33–41; Mark 12:1–9; Luke 20:9–16).

In the parable Jesus refers to his own fate. He understood that his calling was to be the Messiah that God was sending. But in contrast to the expectation that the Messiah would consolidate Israel's political and military power and drive out the foreign oppressors, Jesus announced a kingdom that doesn't come about through force or violence, but in a strange way that looks more like weakness and failure. His own task is to be the "suffering servant" described in chapters forty and following of the book of Isaiah. In these texts a prophet (often called Second Isaiah by scholars) had announced Israel's release from Babylonian captivity, but had used the figure of the suffering servant to describe Israel's God-assigned vocation. Jesus understood the Messiah to be the one who takes up this task on behalf of the people and becomes the agent through whom Israel's calling is decisively accomplished.

NEW TESTAMENT METAPHORS FOR JESUS'S WORK

The New Testament uses various metaphors to describe what was accomplished by Jesus's death on the cross. These include judicial metaphors that speak of judgments of "not guilty" and the removal of penalties. There are also metaphors about a ransom being paid or a debt being removed or a victory being won or a sacrifice being offered. Those who propose theories about the atonement typically take one metaphor or a range of related metaphors and by a process of elaboration develop a specific explanation. But this process often involves extending the metaphors in questionable directions. For example, some early Christian writers started with the idea that the death of Jesus was a ransom and went on to ask who received the ransom. They imagined God as offering some kind of payment to the devil. This account was sometimes combined with the idea that the devil was somehow tricked. It is easy to see how this kind of process of developing a metaphor could lead to fanciful accounts.

While it is a mistake to try to turn a metaphor into a comprehensive theory, it does make sense to ask what truths the various images convey. For example, consider the metaphor of sacrifice, which is vitally important in New Testament thinking about the cross. Jesus's death on the cross reminded Jewish Christians, who were steeped in a religion where the central act of worship involved offering animal sacrifices, of the Jewish sacrificial system. The author of the book of Hebrews sees Jesus as offering the perfect sacrifice that puts an end to the need for further sacrifices. What are we to make of all this talk of Jesus's death as a sacrifice? Should we accept the view of some Christians that God demands blood sacrifices before sins can be forgiven and has finally been satisfied with a human sacrifice?

Doing so, I think, involves a misunderstanding of the meaning of sacrifices in Hebrew Scriptures. In a study of the Jewish sacrificial system Keith Ward concludes that biblical sacrifices are not fundamentally about getting the penalty of sin removed or about appeasing an angry deity. He argues that the sacrifice of an animal is best understood as a symbolic way of offering oneself to God.[2] These acts of devotion serve to renew the worshiper's relationship with God. It is easy to see how such symbolic acts might be perverted. When the prophets criticize the sacrificial system, they sometimes boldly declare that God doesn't care about sacrifices. However, their real target seems to be sacrifices that are performances of a ritual, but disconnected with genuine obedience. Ritual acts are not a substitute for failing to act justly, to love mercy, and to walk humbly with God. Treating them as disconnected from commitment to the kind of life God seeks for us makes them worthless.

If we think of these sacrifices as symbolic ways of offering oneself to God, it is not difficult to see how Jesus's acceptance of the cross could be thought of as a sacrifice. Jesus's self-offering fulfills the deep meaning of the sacrificial system. He offers his life to God and acts in obedience to his call, even when his complete devotion will predictably evoke a hostile response that leads to his crucifixion. He was as one New Testament text says, "obedient to the point of death" (Phil 2:8). But this account still leaves an unanswered question. Why did Jesus need to die when the story of his devotion could have had a different ending, such as a dramatic rescue from those who sought to kill him?

THE CROSS AS A REVELATION OF GOD

I do not claim to know the answer to that question. I could speculate that part of the answer might be connected with the kind of identification with human life God was doing. God was identifying with the depths of pain and suffering that humans face and with the futility they often feel in the face of terrible injustice. A rescue from the worst consequences of human behavior might be viewed as falling short of full identification with the human plight.

But perhaps the explanation goes deeper. Perhaps the cross itself is of central importance for showing us what God is like. Christians agree in taking Jesus's life to be a revelation of the nature of God, indeed the supreme

---

2. Ward, *What the Bible Really Teaches*, 119–24.

revelation of God's nature. When we think of God in the light of how Jesus lived, we see a self-giving love that comes to our aid. But what if it is not just Jesus's life that reveals God's nature, but his death as well? The idea is startling because it conflicts with pictures we have of God's power and how God exercises that power. The cross shows a voluntary refusal on the part of Jesus to defend himself against the forces of evil. He doesn't meet force with force, but instead allows his enemies to do their worst. Surely, we think, that can't be what God is like. We are steeped in images of God stepping in to punish the bad and reward the good. To us, allowing the forces of evil to do their wicked deeds doesn't match what we expect of God. Our heroes are the ones who ride into the lawless town and use force to dispense justice. In fact, our perennial complaint is that God is allowing the wicked to get away with far too much.

But what if God is more like the person described in Jesus's teaching who turns the other cheek when faced with aggression and refuses to respond in kind? What if God responds to those who resist by allowing them to have their way? What if the cross reveals not just what happened once, but the suffering that God continually endures in loving a world that consistently rejects its creator? In an exposition of Paul's discussion of the death of Jesus in Romans, New Testament scholar N. T. Wright suggests that "the overflowing, self-sacrificial love of the Son going to the cross was indeed the accurate and precise expression of the love of God for a world radically out of joint . . ."[3]

However, the problem with thinking in this way is that it suggests to us that God simply lets evil win and doesn't actually come to our aid in the struggle against it. To describe matters in words used by Paul, from every human point of view accepting crucifixion looks like weakness and foolishness. But could it involve, as Paul claims, a deeper wisdom and strength? Wright points toward that possibility when he asserts that the cross of Jesus unleashes a new power to transform our world, the power of self-giving love. He writes,

> The reason the cross carried such life-changing power, and carries it still, is because it embodied, expressed, and symbolized the true power of which all earthly power is either an imitation or a corrupt parody . . . The gospel of Jesus summons us to believe that the power of self-giving love unveiled on the cross is the real thing, the power that made the world in the first place and is now in the business of remaking it; and that other forms

---

3. Wright, *Day the Revolution Began*, 293.

of "power," the corrupt and self-serving ways in which the world is so often run . . . are the distortion.[4]

New Testament writers were convinced that Jesus had somehow defeated the powers that rule this world and brought into existence a new reality. They saw themselves as invited to participate in and to help spread a new kind of life that substitutes forgiveness and service for control and force. The transforming work of self-giving love is slow and involves suffering and setbacks that often look like failure. This way of living also arouses ridicule and opposition from those who are locked into prevailing assumptions about how life works. But the Christian hope is that over time the subversive power of love will prove stronger than the forces that rule this world.

I will discuss in other chapters what it means to think of God as working through the power of love rather than the power of force and violence. However, my primary concern is not to convince you that the way I currently think about the meaning of the cross is the only correct way. Mostly, I am trying to show how rejecting a version of Christian faith that is familiar, but riddled with problems, need not mean abandoning the faith. Instead, it may open a path to deeper insight into what Christian faith is about.

---

4. Wright, *Day the Revolution Began*, 399.

Chapter 10

Being Saved

I GREW UP IN a denomination that had defined itself historically by a rejection of infant baptism. Not only did we Baptists do baptism "the right way" (immersion), we also insisted that baptism should be reserved for those who made their own decision to become Christians. A decision by the parents on behalf of an infant wasn't good enough.

What seems ironic to me now is that while we rejected infant baptism, over the years our churches tended to push back the time when children were expected to make professions of faith and be baptized to increasingly earlier ages. At one point the expected time was during the early teenage years, but eventually decisions from much younger children came to be regarded as standard. This change, I suspect, was connected with the activities of traveling evangelists who conducted meetings we called "revivals" in local churches. It improved their measures of success when they could visit the younger classes and add to their report conversions of children who, though not infants, could hardly be expected to have the kind of understanding our historical forebears presumed to be a condition of making a commitment to Christ.

Those who joined the church in early childhood were taught to describe their experience in ways that conformed to models of salvation that fit more easily with the experiences of adult converts. We were expected to be able to specify a particular time when we were saved and in due course to give a testimony about how we had turned from an old way of life to a new way of life in Christ. There was a decided preference for conversion stories that displayed a sharp contrast between the old way and the new one. I remember hearing testimonies from people who were mired in some sinful habit, such as drug or alcohol abuse, but had repented and changed completely.

I sometimes regretted that I had no such story to tell. It wasn't that I had never done anything bad, but I didn't have any dramatic shift to report. I wasn't like the apostle Paul who had persecuted Christians and then had a pivotal conversion experience that resulted in devoting his life to the spread of Christianity. I was never away from the church or caught up in the kinds of sins that seemed worth highlighting in a testimony. As a result, my story did not fit well with our preferred model of immediate radical change. It was much later that I came to realize that everyone's story did not need to fit into this kind of mold. People can experience the saving work of Christ in many ways, not just the particularly dramatic forms we idealized.

The churches I attended were significantly shaped by a nineteenth-century revivalist tradition that emphasized public professions of faith. Our church services, like the evangelistic meetings featured in that tradition, always ended with an invitation hymn, during which you could "walk the aisle" to the front of the church and accept Christ. The invitation hymn was often accompanied by exhortations between verses to "come forward." The hymn was routinely extended to additional verses to make sure that no one who needed to respond lacked opportunity. I remember hearing stories warning about people who put off the decision and then died in a traffic accident before they could get another chance. There was anxiety over the possibility that we might be closing the invitation too soon.

Every sermon, no matter what the topic or text, eventually focused on what we called "being saved." Other matters might be brought up, but it was assumed that nothing was more important than appealing to those who urgently needed to make a decision for Christ. This emphasis made these sermons somewhat irrelevant to people who had already joined the church, except perhaps that there were sermons that raised the question of whether the salvation you thought you had was genuine. In our tradition, the belief was that you couldn't be saved more than once, but you could mistakenly think you were converted and later experience real conversion. This possibility meant that people might walk the aisle multiple times to be sure that they were right with God. The invitation was also open to people who felt things weren't quite right, so they needed to "rededicate" their lives.

Our focus on the initial salvation experience led us, I think, to neglect meaningful instruction about how to live the Christian life. There was relatively little attention given to spiritual growth or everyday discipleship. I don't remember hearing much about what it meant in practical terms to love your neighbor, and nothing at all about loving your enemies. We were urged, of course, to read our Bibles and to pray, but the emphasis wasn't on what I later came to call spiritual formation. The messages I heard that related to how to live were mostly preaching against overt behaviors that our churches frowned on, such as drinking or illicit sex or other activities deemed worldly. The implicit communication that many of us took in was that you were okay if you had been saved and you refrained from doing things on the bad list.

The urgency we felt about getting people saved arose from our conception of the connection between salvation to what would happen after death. You needed to be saved because God would judge you, and unless you had accepted Christ, that judgment would not go well. It was all a bit scary, for the stakes were understood to be about where you would spend eternity. You would either go to heaven or hell, and your fate depended on whether you had prayed the right prayer or sincerely said the right words in time.

After I made my decision to accept Jesus at the age of six, I recall going to my parents one night in fear that my little sister (two years younger) would be going to hell because she had not yet made a profession of faith. My parents tried to reassure me that my sister would be okay because she had not yet reached the "age of accountability." I don't remember whether their reassurances helped, but in retrospect this account seems to me to project our legalistic construal of things onto God. I now view the ideas about being saved I grew up with as a simplistic distortion of the biblical message.

A FLAWED PICTURE OF SALVATION

Our understanding of what would happen after death limited the way we could think about salvation. Believing that going to heaven depended on having an identifiable salvation experience meant that we needed to think of salvation as something that happened at a specific moment. There had to be a decisive answer at any given point in time to the question of whether you were saved or not. Otherwise, how could it be determined when you died what your eternal destiny would be? So, we could not entertain the idea that salvation might be more of a process than an event. A person was either saved or not, and there wasn't any in-between. We did not consider the possibility that a person's relationship with God might be more complicated than this sharp dichotomy could accommodate, nor did we consider the possibility that everything did not need to be definitively settled at death. If someone had brought up such ideas, we would have said that they went against clear biblical teaching. It wasn't that we thought that after the event of salvation there was no need for spiritual development, but we could not view salvation itself as less than fully achieved. We needed to keep the issue of whether any transformation had occurred or was occurring separate from the issue of whether some event had resulted in your name being written in the book of life.

Our focus on the connection between being saved and going to heaven made it easy for us to miss how often biblical authors describe salvation in terms of immediate this-worldly benefits. For example, in the Gospels Jesus frequently represents gaining release from some physical affliction as a sign of salvation. He repeatedly tells those who are cured, "Your faith has saved you." He uses the same phrase in connection with forgiveness of sins, which he seems to treat as a part of his healing ministry. In other words, salvation is described as occurring when someone achieves release from physical or spiritual barriers to well-being. Some translators render Jesus's phrase about faith saving you as, "Your faith has made you whole." This translation is apt because making people whole is what salvation does. Salvation in the Gospels is about having our capacities working as they should so that we are freed to live as we were intended to live. Admittedly, the term "salvation" is also used in the New Testament in relation to the ultimate destiny of Christians, but that destiny should be thought of as continuous with the therapeutic work God initiates in this life. The biblical view of salvation is distorted when we construe it as a ticket to heaven that can be treated as separate from the transformative results that are the point of salvation.

Our focus on going to heaven also disposed us to think of salvation as an individual good and to miss its connection to communal life. During Jesus's visit with a tax collector named Zacchaeus, the tax collector declares his intention to give half his possessions to the poor and to pay back four times the amount he has defrauded from anyone. Jesus responds, "Today salvation has come to this house because he too is a son of Abraham" (Luke 19:9). Apparently, the signs of Zacchaeus's salvation are a shift in his attitudes toward others and a willingness to use his money differently, and these changes allow him to be restored to the Jewish community. This tax collector who has been thought of as a traitor to his own people can now be received as a son of Abraham. In biblical thought salvation is not just a good for an individual to enjoy alone. Being saved is inseparable from participation in a communal life where God's purposes for human beings can be achieved.

Another major problem with our understanding of salvation was that it was in tension with the biblical teaching that God loved us. We were told, of course, that God loved us, but we were also told that those who failed to accept God's salvation would be punished harshly. We might not have said so, but God's willingness to follow through on these threats did not seem like love. When young people in the kinds of churches I attended reached an age when they could think about these matters, they typically raised questions about what God would do about those who hadn't accepted Jesus, maybe because they hadn't heard the Gospel message or maybe because they had been brought up in a culture or a religion that kept them from taking Christian teachings seriously. It was hard to avoid the suspicion that our way of thinking led to a view of God as arbitrary and unfair, rather than loving and just. But if someone had suggested that anyone could be saved apart from the kind of acceptance of Jesus that was central in our teaching and practice, the worry was that we would be denying what the Bible taught.

I would say now that the rigidness of our theology got in the way of hearing the biblical message of God's love, and it certainly got in the way of thinking that God loved those who did not share our beliefs. The problem was not with having a doctrine of salvation. It was rather with understanding salvation primarily in terms of what happens after death and construing the conditions for salvation in such a way that most people would be excluded. It was hard to take seriously biblical proclamations that God desires the salvation of all, when things were apparently set up in such a way that only a few would enjoy God's rewards and the rest would suffer excruciating punishment.

AN ALTERNATIVE VIEW

An alternative to thinking of salvation primarily in terms of receiving a heavenly reward or avoiding the punishments of hell is to think of it as a kind of fulfillment of our nature. God's offer of salvation can be understood as an offer to turn us into people who are fully capable of loving and experiencing the joys of love. In other words, it is an offer of the kind of abundant life that God wants us to have. If we think in these terms, it does not seem surprising that salvation might be a process, rather than something that occurs in an instant. Receiving the gift of salvation may involve significant transformative events, but it also involves continuing to consent to have God do in you the kind of transforming work that makes you more Christlike.

Once we appreciate the connection between salvation and the sort of fulfillment God seeks for us, we can see why God's desire for our salvation is an expression of God's love. According to Scripture, God's love extends to everyone. Taking seriously the biblical teaching that God desires the salvation of all, however, leads to questions about some of the teachings I grew up with that seem to limit the scope of salvation. For example, is

God's transforming work available only to those who have accepted central Christian teachings? Also, is a person's fate fixed at death?

I was taught that salvation was only for people who had acquired the right beliefs. If you accepted some other set of religious beliefs or if you had no religious beliefs, you were out of luck. But if we think that God desires the salvation of everyone, we have some reason to expect God's transforming work to extend beyond the limited number of people who have accepted core Christian teachings. Perhaps God can do more to transform people who have a fuller grasp of central revelatory truths, but surely God's desire to make us into creatures who fully love can at least begin with people whose grasp of truth is partial or confused.

If an atheist denies God's existence, but is responsive to the pull of a sense of goodness, might that atheist be responding to God without realizing it? If someone has warped religious ideas, would that confusion keep God from starting a work of transformation that could culminate eventually in making this person fit for a heavenly kind of existence? My point here is not that beliefs do not matter or that there is no advantage in having accurate beliefs. It is rather that taking seriously God's love for all means extending God's saving work beyond people who manage to develop a good theology. Someone can be on a path that leads eventually to full redemption even if that person does not know it. One positive consequence of this way of thinking is that it undermines the all-too-common tendency among Christians to view outsiders with attitudes that are divisive and unloving. Self-righteous condescension is harder to maintain when we no longer confidently think that we can pronounce people who differ from us to be rejected by God.

But to think that God's saving work is more extensive than many of us have acknowledged and to recognize that this work is a process raises the question of how long such a process extends. I was taught that everything had to be finalized at the point of death. But why can't God's transformative work extend beyond death? Some Christians are willing to acknowledge that when they die, further spiritual development will still be needed. Shouldn't we also think that when God has begun a process that could with enough time bring someone who hasn't accepted Christianity to the kind of fulfillment God seeks, the process can continue beyond death?

Some would say we cannot consider such an idea because the Bible teaches otherwise. I am not convinced it does. I find no clear biblical teaching on the issue. It is certainly not decided by the verse that says, "it is appointed for mortals to die once, and after that the judgment" (Heb 9:27). But even if there is no decisive biblical pronouncement on the matter, reflection on clear teachings about God that are in the Bible may lead us to doubt that everything is decided at death. Would the God Jesus described, who goes to extraordinary lengths to save us, instantly stop such efforts when extending the process might still lead to a positive outcome? If learning particular truths is important to completing the process, then couldn't God provide opportunities for learning these truths to those who failed to do so during their earthly lives?

But in that case, where is the motivation for trying to spread the gospel message? Some people think that such motivation is undermined if we allow for the possibility of responding to God after death. I don't see why. If you think that you know something about how to live the best kind of life, doesn't that give you a motivation to try to share it? If you believe that the biblical revelation of God's love in Christ is true, wouldn't you want others to discover that truth? Even if you think that without your efforts, others might eventually learn these life-changing truths, wouldn't you want people to learn them sooner rather than later?

I will put off until the next chapter the question of how to understand divine judgment. Here I will only suggest that the view of salvation I was taught was bound up with ideas about punishment in the afterlife that now seem to me a distortion of the Christian message. The doctrine of hell that our understanding of salvation presupposed was presented as just what the Bible taught on the subject. But we had learned to read the Bible with an expectation that it confirmed the doctrines we held, and we were unprepared to do serious thinking about whether our interpretations were correct. What stands out to me now is that to accept the ideas about God's judgment and punishment we were taught, we had to think in ways that might have been conducive to responding to God in fear, but were not at all conducive to responding with love.

SALVATION AND DISCIPLESHIP

In the churches where I grew up, salvation was our preferred term for being properly related to God. But it is not the only biblical term. A central New Testament term is discipleship. The original disciples included people who responded to the call to leave their fishing nets and follow Jesus, which literally meant going where he went and becoming a part of his mission. We can't follow in the way they did, but we can still think of the Christian life in terms of joining the mission that Jesus calls us to and taking direction from his instructions. When we think of ourselves as disciples of Jesus, we can see clearly the need for continuing commitment to follow a path that may be very difficult. The idea of discipleship focuses our attention on living the Christian life, not just on its beginning or culmination.

The single-minded emphasis on being saved in the churches where I grew up tended to eclipse the importance of other biblical terms, such as discipleship. But it is instructive to imagine how our thinking might have differed if we had framed the issue of relationship with God in terms of being disciples of Jesus. Rather than worrying much about whether and precisely when the process started, we might have thought it more important to ask, "Are you a disciple now?" Rather than thinking that the important thing had already happened when we walked a church aisle, we might have recognized the centrality of the way of living Jesus outlines for his followers. Rather than thinking that our primary concern should be with what happens after death, attention to Jesus's teaching might have shifted our focus to what God is trying to do in this world and how we can participate in it.

Using a range of biblical terms to think about our relationship with God can help us guard against an unduly narrow way of conceiving the Christian message. There is no problem in thinking that sometimes God's work involves decisive events. The problem is rather that emphasizing a single event exclusively can result in missing the fuller picture. It is as if someone imagines that once the wedding has occurred, the marriage will take care of itself.

If I had concluded that the way I was initially taught to think about salvation was the only option, I likely would have given up on being a Christian. But fortunately, through exposure to a wider range of Christian thought, I became aware of ways to understand salvation other than the truncated view I had been taught. As a result, I was able to reshape my understanding of Christianity in ways that made Christian faith make sense to me. My rethinking did not mean disregarding what the Bible says. If anything, it meant having blinders that restricted the way I understood biblical texts removed. In the end changing my mind turned out to be a way of preserving my faith.

Chapter 11

Divine Judgment and Punishment

Some of the ways God is described as acting in the Bible are pretty scary. Biblical texts report that God repeatedly becomes angry and lashes out in violent ways. Sometimes the result is destruction of whole cities (e.g., Gen 19). In one case all of human life except for a single family is wiped out (Gen 6–7). God strikes down the first-born child of Egyptian families (Exod 15), sends plagues and famines that kill thousands (Num 16, 25; 2 Sam 21, 24), and uses enemy armies to bring devastating destruction on Israel (e.g., 2 Kgs 13). If we take these stories to heart, we can't help but find God's judgment to be a fearful prospect.

I was taught as a young boy that biblical references to "the fear of God" should not be understood to mean literally being afraid. Teachers told me they meant we should respect and honor God. No doubt references to the fear of God in Scripture sometimes have that meaning, but believing in an agent as powerful as God who can be provoked to violent responses was surely a source of actual fear for ancient Israelites. Biblical texts sometimes convey a sense of awe in the presence of God, but they also say that that people were terrified to get too close to manifestations of God lest they die. Even when the reaction is not terror, fear of the consequences of God's disapproval is evident. Biblical wisdom writers who say we should fear God clearly thought that it was a mark of wisdom to be deterred from bad behavior by the prospect of divine retribution.

Sometimes the consequences of disobedience are spelled out in graphic detail. For example, in Deut 28:15–68 we find an extended account of what will happen to the people of Israel if they don't heed God's commands. A summary passage says, "The Lord will send upon you disaster, panic, and frustration in everything you attempt to do, until you are destroyed . . ." (28:20). In the list of disasters threatened are disease epidemics, crop failures, and conquest by enemies. The consequences of these calamities, we are told, include people becoming mad, going blind, and even eating their own children to stave off starvation. After the Babylonian conquest, the book of Lamentations repeatedly underlines the message of multiple prophets that the extreme suffering that has come upon the nation is something that God has done to them: "The Lord has done what he purposed, he has carried out his threat . . . he has demolished without pity" (Lam 2:17).

The same Bible that describes God as bringing suffering and death also says that God loves us. But if we accept the stories of God angrily bringing destruction on those who disobey, the kind of love God has for humans seems conditional. It feels as if God loves you when you do the right things, but brings extreme punishment on you when you don't toe the line. The picture of God as a harsh disciplinarian can easily overwhelm any sense of comfort that we might gain from the declaration that God loves us. We might affirm that a human father whose outbursts of anger make us walk on eggshells loves us in some sense, but it is not the kind of love we long for, and if a human father's anger led to the kind of suffering God is described as inflicting, we would not call it love at all.

DOING AND ALLOWING

At times biblical writers offer revisions to some of the ways divine judgment is described. In 2 Sam 24 we are told that "the anger of the Lord was kindled against Israel, and he incited David against them" by instructing David to take a census (2 Sam 24:1). David follows God's order, but later comes to believe that doing the census was wrong, a conclusion that is confirmed when a prophet announces that there will be punishment. According to the account, God sends a "pestilence on Israel," which results in the death of seventy thousand people. After this pestilence, God relents from further punishment and stops an angelic agent from proceeding to destroy Jerusalem. So, according to the account, God incites David to do wrong and then kills seventy thousand people because of what David has done. When the author of 1 Chronicles tells the same story, it is revised to say that it was Satan who incited David to take the census (1 Chr 21:1). Apparently, the later writer rejects the idea that God incites people to do wrong—just as the book of James later rejects the idea that God tempts people (Jas 1:13–14).

Nevertheless, the Chronicles account still reports that God sends a pestilence that kills seventy thousand people and that divine punishment is stopped just short of destroying Jerusalem.

By the time we get to the writings of Paul, it is not just the idea of God inciting people to do wrong that is being rethought. We find a change in how the cause of devastation is described. The book of Numbers describes God as sending plagues because of various sins. However, when Paul refers to these stories in First Corinthians, he is careful to describe what killed people as "serpents" and "the destroyer" (1 Cor 10:9–11). Just as the writer of Chronicles has introduced an agent other than God as the one who incites wrongdoing, Paul refers to intermediary causes of the plagues. His way of describing these events suggests reluctance to attribute horrific suffering directly to God.

But is this difference important? After all, even if the source of temptation or destruction involves powers other than God, doesn't God allow those powers to operate? Admittedly so, but if we think that God has reasons for giving these powers some degree of independence, we don't have to think of the mass destruction as sent by God. Saying that God creates a natural order in which hurricanes and plagues can kill people is not the same as saying that God sends hurricanes and plagues in order to kill people. Saying that Jack killed Jill is not equivalent to saying that God used Jack to kill Jill. Conceiving of what happens in terms of secondary causes opens the door to thinking that the natural order or finite agents may produce some results that God does not seek or endorse.

Some of the acts biblical writers ascribe to God look different when we think of what happens in terms of secondary causes. For example, when Exodus tells us that God hardened Pharaoh's heart against freeing the Israelites, it sounds as if Pharaoh is a helpless pawn in a game where God produces Pharaoh's resistance and then sends the plagues as a response to it, but if we can imagine that what God does is to allow Pharaoh to harden his own heart, we can think differently about the story. Scholars tell us that biblical writers often don't make a distinction between what God causes directly and what God allows to happen. Where they might describe a plague as sent by God, we might attribute the plague to the functioning of a natural order that generally works for human good, but sometimes results in death and destruction. Our use of distinctions that biblical authors do not make is sometimes taken to mean that when those authors describe God as bringing about massive suffering, their descriptions are not in conflict with ours. But that characterization can be misleading. If we imagine not having the distinctions that enable us to say God did not cause these events, we are left with portrayals that most of us find deeply troubling.

DOES GOD BRING CALAMITY?

Distinguishing between what God causes directly and what God allows does not by itself settle the question of whether God is correctly described as sending plagues, hurricanes or enemy armies in order to destroy. Someone could say that the various secondary causes are ways that God brings destruction. Some well-known television evangelists have spoken in this way when they describe particular natural disasters and terrorist acts as divine judgment for types of sins that they seem confident they can identify.[1] One reason for questioning such accounts is that it seems farfetched to think that natural disasters or acts of terrorism kill only those people most deserving of punishment. The appearances suggest that that harm comes indiscriminately to guilty and innocent people alike. So, attributing these acts to God suggests that God does not care whether there are innocent victims, which makes God's behavior seem monstrous.

There is also an opposite problem when we think of God as using natural forces as punishment. It is that many of the people who most deserve judgment do not seem to get this kind of retribution. If we think that God sends plagues to strike down people who do wrong, then why does God refrain from sending a plague to stop some of the cruelest of perpetrators? When we look honestly at the way the world works, the model of God maintaining the moral order by zapping evildoers who get out of line seems implausible as a description of how God governs the world.

The problem, however, is not just that the distribution of suffering through natural calamities or horrendous human acts raises questions about God enacting justice through such events. There is something about the idea of an angry deity sending awful suffering to people that is hard to square with biblical claims about God's love. If we imagine these acts in the way biblical writers often portray them as motivated by anger rather than love, we seem to be attributing competing motives to God. God loves us and often acts for our good, but at times gets angry enough at us to destroy us. We could alter this picture by claiming that the attributions of anger in these accounts are not to be taken literally, but are instead poetic ways of describing God's acts. However, this alteration by itself still leaves the question of how a loving God, even if not literally angry, could send such suffering.

But if we reject the idea that God inflicts suffering in the way biblical texts describe, what should we say about these accounts? The best approach, I think, is to view accounts in Hebrew Scriptures as part of a long process by which Israel comes to know God and to acknowledge that at some stages

---

1. Jonathan Merritt discusses the response of Jerry Falwell and Pat Robertson to the events of 9-11 in *Faith of Our Own*, 49-53.

of the process biblical writers presume primitive ideas about God that need to be corrected in the light of fuller revelation. It is understandable why ancient Israelite writers portrayed God as bringing violent retribution. That was the way all the nations they knew about described their gods. Borrowing imagery from other ancient Near Eastern religions, biblical writers sometimes attempt to glorify God as a bloodthirsty warrior who ruthlessly brings vengeance on all who offer opposition. They sometimes describe God as acting with all the pettiness and vindictiveness that kings of this era regularly exhibited. In other words, they describe God by means of the cultural vocabulary that was available to them.[2]

Some Christians think that if the Bible says that God did it, God must have done it, and there is no way to question whether God acted as described. But in so doing, they make it easy for critics of biblical religion who also take these descriptions at face value, but issue pointed indictments of the deity they portray. Richard Dawkins comments acidly,

> The God of the Old Testament is arguably the most unpleasant character in all fiction: jealous and proud of it; a petty, unjust, unforgiving control-freak; a vindictive, bloodthirsty, ethnic cleanser; a misogynistic, homophobic, racist, infanticidal, genocidal, sadomasochistic, capriciously malevolent bully.[3]

Admittedly, the characterization is a one-sided and uncharitable reading of these texts, but when hostile critics read biblical accounts as exact renditions of what happened, it is understandable that they might find some grounds for disgust. When God is described as doing despicable things, we ought to feel some disgust as well.

The best reply to such critics is not to try to defend all the actions attributed to God, but rather to admit that objectionable biblical portrayals of God are part of a very messy process. Some scriptural texts contain primitive and confused ideas arising from assumptions of the time that can be judged deficient from the perspective of a reflective awareness that was not available until later. There is room for disagreement about what exactly should be discarded and what should be retained. But Christians ought to agree that characterizations of God that do not fit with the revelation of God in Christ should be rejected.

---

2. Boyd, *Cross Vision*, 121–32.
3. Dawkins, *God Delusion*, 51.

RETHINKING PUNISHMENT

If we think that the way scriptural texts sometimes describe God's judgment is defective, do we need to reject the idea of divine punishment altogether? Not necessarily, though we may need to revise the way we understand it. Multiple writers have distinguished between different types of punishment. I'll use Gregory Boyd's terms. He distinguishes between judicial punishment and organic punishment.[4] For an example of judicial punishment, think of a judge sending someone to prison for robbery. In one sense going to prison is a consequence of doing the robbery, but that is because we have set up a system in which particular crimes are assigned particular types of punishment that are enforced by an external authority. The other kind of punishment is what Boyd calls organic punishment. The idea is that there are negative consequences that are natural results of particular ways of acting. For example, when we give in to some kinds of passions, we acquire addictions that weaken our ability to control our own lives. When we disregard the needs or interests of others, we weaken our capacity for empathetic reactions needed to participate in a healthy community. When we procrastinate doing what we know is needed, we end up unprepared.

Often when people think of God punishing, they are imagining a judicial punishment. You have broken the rules, so I'll send an earthquake to kill you or a devastating disease to make your life miserable or a plunge in the stock markets to weaken your financial security. God is conceived as an enforcer of the rules. Suppose, however, that we think in terms of organic punishment. God's punishment, conceived in this way, is to let you suffer the consequences of what you have done. While there are places in the Bible where the judicial model is used to think of God's punishment, it is striking how often it is described in terms that fit better with an organic model. In Rom 1 Paul speaks of the wrath of God being revealed "against all ungodliness and wickedness" (1:18). He refers to idolatry and to degrading lusts. What is it that God does to those sinners? In verse 24 Paul says "God gave them up" to their depravities. Twice more in the same passage (verses 26 and 28) Paul repeats the phrase "God gave them up." So, what is the punishment he is envisioning? It sounds as if the punishment of these acts is that God lets people suffer the consequences of the way of life they have chosen.[5]

Boyd writes, "Contrary to what many people think, the Bible generally construes God's punishment of sin as *organic* in nature. God doesn't *impose*

---

4. Boyd, *Cross Vision*, 148–49.
5. For a helpful discussion of Paul's reworking of divine wrath see Jersak, *More Christlike God*, 204–10.

punishments on people. The destructive consequences of sin are *built into the sin itself*."[6] It is possible to dispute whether divine punishment is always organic rather than judicial, but Boyd is correct in recognizing that sin is frequently represented as bringing its own punishment. In Ps 7, for example, the evildoers are pictured as digging a hole and falling into it (7:15). Those who practice violence discover that it falls "on their own head" (Ps 7:16).

Even if both ways of thinking about divine punishment can be found in the Bible, we can ask whether one of the two better represents the revelation of God we find in Jesus. Jesus taught that when we love our enemies, we are acting as God does when God sends good things indiscriminately to all (Matt 5:44–45). In Luke's account of Jesus's teaching, we are told to be merciful so we can be like God who is "kind to the ungrateful and wicked" (Luke 6:35–36). In one Gospel story Jesus explicitly rejects the suggestion of his disciples to summon fire from heaven to destroy those who did not receive him (Luke 9:54). He does take the opportunity to call out evil, both verbally and in symbolic ways, such as turning over tables of moneychangers in the temple. But if Jesus shows us what God is like, we do not get the impression of a strong concern to make sure wrongdoers are properly penalized. Even when his enemies bring about his death, he prays for their forgiveness. I think that his teaching and his life should incline us in the direction of thinking that God's punishment is more organic than judicial. If we add our observations about what happens to evildoers in this world, we find additional reasons to think that God does not act in the way the judicial model would lead us to expect.

BUT WHAT ABOUT HELL?

Even if Jesus did not deliver punishment to the wicked, doesn't the Bible teach that God will later bring this kind of judgment by sentencing some people to eternal torment in hell? Bradley Jersak is a theologian who describes himself as an evangelical Christian. But he rejects some of the evangelical teachings he grew up with, including the claim that God will sentence some people to eternal conscious torment. In a careful study of the issue, Jersak deals with biblical teachings on the subject, as well as the teachings of significant historical and contemporary Christian thinkers. His analysis of New Testament texts that relate to the idea of hell shows why interpreting these texts is a complex task that calls for awareness of the linguistic and historical background of relevant passages, as well as sensitivity to symbolic meanings. Some passages that have been understood as teachings about life

---

6. Boyd, *Cross Vision*, 148–49.

after death are better understood as descriptions of how militant resistance to Rome will lead to the destruction of Jerusalem. Some passages refer to suffering after death that can be understood as temporary and therapeutic, rather than punitive. Jersak also calls attention to a range of biblical texts that lead us to expect the eventual salvation of everyone.

In addition to what the Bible teaches, Jersak points out that a number of early church fathers accepted the view that in the end God would prevail and all will be saved. On his account, it was largely the influence of Augustine in the fourth century that solidified support for the alternative view that some are predestined to heaven, but others will suffer eternal torment in hell. Jersak does not claim that the teaching of universal salvation can be demonstrated to be the correct view, but he does embrace a hope that in the end all will be saved. His book concludes with a discussion of Rev 21–22. He finds in these chapters something surprising. The wicked who have received their punishment can come into the heavenly city by washing their robes in the blood of the lamb. The text specifically says that the gates of the city will never be shut. From this passage Jersak takes the title of his book on hell: *Her Gates Will Never Be Shut*.[7]

My own expertise is not as a biblical scholar, but as a philosopher. One traditional philosophical issue is called the problem of evil. It is the question of how a supremely good and all-powerful God could allow so much suffering. You don't have to be a philosopher to ask that question. It has troubled many ordinary Christians, sometimes resulting in an inability to continue believing the Christian message. But it is often not recognized that eternal punishment in hell would be part of the problem of evil. Would a loving God allow extreme suffering that goes on forever and leads to no good outcome? Most philosophers who consider this question answer no. Those who defend the idea that God could allow something that can be called hell invariably connect such a state to God's refusal to overrule human freedom.

In a discussion of the problem of evil C. S. Lewis claims that the only kind of hell God allows is the kind we freely choose. "The doors of hell," he says picturesquely, are "locked on the *inside*."[8] In a fantasy novel he imagines residents of the "city" that represents life apart from God visiting the outskirts of heaven.[9] They can stay if they choose. But most of those who visit decide to go back because drawing close to the Love that is the source of all things inevitably means leaving behind things that cannot be combined with the way of love. Lewis's picture of people trying to make a

7. Jersak, *Her Gates Will Never Be Shut*, 165–79.
8. Lewis, *Problem of Pain*, 127.
9. Lewis, *Great Divorce*, 122–23.

life apart from God suggests that as we move farther away from God, we are moving away from the reality that holds us together as persons. If this way of life is what we choose, he thinks, God allows us to have it. Notice that on this account hell is not so much a sentence imposed on us, but the organic punishment of getting the consequences of the way of life we insist upon.

Even if we reject a view of hell as unrelenting torture that has no redemptive purpose as inconsistent with the love of God, we can still take seriously biblical warnings about suffering that might occur after death. Some suffering may in fact be required because of God's love. Imagine that you have gone into the afterlife. To be made fit for God's presence, you need to face up to reality, but among the habits of earthly existence is the habit of creating false realities in which we excuse or do not even recognize our own evil deeds. We get used to seeing things exclusively from our own self-serving point of view. What we need is something to shock us out of our rationalizations. Imagine watching a replay of some event from your earthly life in which you acted with cruelty, but now imagine experiencing the event from the point of view of your victims. The pain involved in recognizing what you have done might be a necessary part of choosing to embrace God's point of view, rather than clinging to your own fictions.

On this picture of things, the path to redemption may involve suffering, but the suffering is integrally connected with the transformation needed for life in the kind of community that reflects divine love. If we finally resist the kind of transformation we need, perhaps because we find it too painful, then the alternative is to try to make a life apart from God. But to succeed at this task is to be in hell, which we might think of not so much as a place we are sent, but a way of life we won't let go of. Conceivably this consequence may not even be hell from the perspective of those who choose it, but only from the perspective of those who have tasted of something better.

GOD'S DELIGHT

In one of my previous churches the pastor offered a blessing to the congregation each week that included these words: "May the God who loves you take delight in your living." I found the words striking because they suggested a way of thinking about God that did not fit well with views I had acquired in my formative years. I had learned to picture God as a demanding judge who was quick to correct and slow to praise. I had come to think that God was not going to be satisfied with my feeble efforts to do the right thing, much less my willful rebellion. I could ask for forgiveness, and God would graciously give it. But even if God accepted me, my flaws, I assumed, overshadowed any good qualities I might possess.

The picture of God as a demanding judge who looks at humans with a critical eye makes the idea that God might actually delight in my living seem farfetched. Notice, however, that in the pastor's blessing, the delight God might take is connected with God's love. What does the oft-repeated phrase that God loves us mean? Is it only a grudging acceptance? That does not sound much like love. What would we think of a parent whose concern with correcting the faults of her children was so great that she was never able to find any enjoyment in their uniqueness? Enjoyment looks like a natural expression of love, and not finding anything to enjoy suggests not genuinely valuing and, hence, not genuinely loving.

What if we could replace the picture of God as obsessed with penalizing our failures with the picture of God finding delight in the baby steps we take toward our good? What if we could remind ourselves that the son who has insisted on going into the far country has a Father who is more eager to throw a party to celebrate his return than to offer a rebuke? Such a shift might enable us to let go of some of the fears that cloud our vision of God's love and to open our hearts to a joyful response.

Chapter 12

Is God in Control of Everything?

I HAVE OFTEN HEARD people say with great confidence, "Everything happens for a reason." One of my former colleagues, a philosopher at a university where I used to teach, told me that he was surprised how often he heard this claim from students. He said that his usual response when a student affirmed the idea during class discussion was to ask, "Why do you think so?" His skepticism may have been apparent, but he refrained from saying during class what he told me privately: the view seemed so absurd to him that he could not understand how anyone could believe it.

What do people mean when they say that everything happens for a reason? I suspect that the kind of reason they have in mind is what we see in events that initially seem undesirable or perhaps just random, but turn out to fit into a larger pattern where they can be recognized as contributing to some good result. For instance, you miss your ride to work one day and discover that the delay enables you to help a friend who had been contemplating suicide. Or you get into an auto accident that sends you to a hospital where a diagnostic test reveals a cancerous condition you didn't know about, but which is now treatable because it was picked up early. Or in the longer term, imagine having a childhood where you had to do something you hated, such as frequently moving to new places, but later came to view these experiences as valuable preparation for a career you love. When people consider outcomes like these, they sometimes find it hard to resist thinking that what happened was somehow arranged.

Nobody denies that what initially seems bad can turn out to be good, but to say that *everything* happens for a reason is not just claiming that this sort of thing *sometimes* occurs. It says that *no events* are just bad or meaningless. They all fit into this kind of pattern. People who think in this way are sometimes confident there is a reason for why someone lost a spouse or was hit by a drunk driver or got fired from a job. Sometimes they offer ideas about what the reason might be. But even when they don't, they may feel sure that there must be a larger pattern that makes sense of what has happened.

This confidence is unlikely to arise just from observing events. I think people who hold this view usually derive it from their thinking about God being in control of things. They imagine God as behind the scenes pulling the strings to bring about unexpected results in accordance with a comprehensive plan. People often find the belief that the events of our lives fit into such a plan comforting, especially when they face difficult circumstances. Saying that everything happens for a reason is often a way of suggesting that when we find ourselves in despair about what seems bad or senseless, we need to look for the bigger picture that can transform our assessment of its meaning.

But despite the comfort some people get from thinking that everything fits into a larger plan, that idea leads to a problem for people who believe in God. To view whatever happens as being in accordance with a divine plan, you have to imagine God arranging for some pretty awful things to happen. You may have no problem with thinking that God makes you late for work some day because your presence is desperately needed elsewhere, but it is another thing altogether to think that God arranges for you to be raped so that you can demonstrate your graciousness by forgiving the offender or that God gives your child cancer to get you to recognize you are too obsessed with business success. Someone might respond that it is not a matter of God causing these bad things, but only allowing them to happen. However, if God's plan is for the bad thing to occur, does it really matter whether God causes it directly or uses secondary means to bring it about?

People often blame God for allowing bad things to happen. "Why," they say, "did God let me be born with a genetic disease that will gradually take away my ability to control my body?" Or "Why did God let my spouse get a gambling addiction that ruined the family finances?" Or "Why did God let a tornado destroy my home?" Answers can be given to the question of why such things occur, but seeing the terrible events of life as part of God's plan makes the most plausible answers irrelevant. It doesn't help to say that the natural order is what caused a debilitating disease if God's plan is to make use of the natural order to infect someone. It doesn't help to talk about free will if God has arranged for a particular misuse of free will in order to achieve some larger purpose. In short, when we magnify God's role in shaping whatever happens, we also magnify God's responsibility for awful things that occur.

DOES GOD CHOOSE FOR BAD THINGS TO HAPPEN?

Believing that God is in total control seems to some Christians not just a comfort, but absolutely vital to their faith. One reason is their fear that anything less than total control would weaken their assurance that God's purposes will be achieved. Another is that it just seems impious to some to think that anything is beyond God's control. People who believe God controls everything that happens do not always understand this control to mean that God actually wills particular bad things to happen. But sometimes they embrace this conclusion.

John Piper, a popular preacher and author who accepts a Calvinist theology that emphasizes divine sovereignty, speaks as follows about the events of 9/11:

> After the planes flew into the Twin Towers in New York, I was interviewed and people would ask me, "Where was God in this?" I said, "Well, God could have very easily blown those planes off course by a little puff of wind, and he didn't do it. Therefore God was right there ordaining that this happen, because he could have stopped it just like that."[1]

Piper goes on to say, "The sovereignty of God, while creating problems for his involvement in sin and evil, is the very rock-solid foundation that allows us to carry on in life." Believing that God has control over all events is needed, he says, to "help us deal with the very evils he has ordained to come into our lives . . ."[2]

Piper's view is that God could prevent any evil, but sometimes chooses for evil things to come about. However, even if it makes us uncomfortable to think of God as ordaining terrible events, Piper says we should not consider questioning whether God decides which evils occur because believing in this kind of control enables us to face our difficulties with confidence in God's power to aid us. I don't find this argument persuasive. You don't have to think that God is controlling everything that happens to believe that God can help when you face difficulties, and thinking that God intentionally brings some difficulties into your life makes it harder to rely on God for

1. Piper, "How Can Evil," lines 28–32.
2. Piper, "How Can Evil," lines 48–51.

help. How can I welcome God's comfort for the loss of my spouse if God was the one who decided that my spouse would become sick and die? How can I appreciate any help that might be given if my need for help arises only because God has sent the problem in the first place? How can I even be confident that the one who sends suffering my way wants to help?

To his credit, Piper acknowledges that there is a problem in attributing to God the kind of control he ascribes because it means thinking of God as very much involved in ordaining sin and evil. But consider how massive this problem is. If we think that God ordains every evil that occurs in the world, we have to say that God ordained the destruction of six million Jews during World War II, along with all other cases of genocidal killing. We would also have to say that God ordains it whenever someone gets tortured or raped or maimed. We would have to conceive of God as ordaining each case of starvation or drowning or child molestation. If we are unwilling to say such things, we need to think about the kind of control God has in a different way.

I don't mean to suggest that those who think God ordains each of these events believe that God is unconcerned with the suffering in the world. Generally, they think God is ordering what happens in such a way as to produce an overall good, and unfortunately achieving the good means accepting a great many evil things. However, once you start to think of God managing things in this way, the complaints of all those who find God blameworthy for terrible things that happen gain considerable force. God might have prevented the kidnapper from holding your young daughter captive to use her for his sexual enjoyment, but thought that some greater good would come from letting it all happen. Would you find any claim about some good this atrocity might lead to a justification for choosing it to occur?

It is difficult to hold onto the idea that God is good and also to accept the claim that each evil in the world is what God ordains. In fact, a significant reason why some people find they can no longer believe in God is that they don't see how they can reconcile the awful things that happen in our world with the claim that a perfectly benevolent God is in control. It is hard to avoid the impression that God, conceived in this way, does not exist.

CREATION AND DIVINE CONTROL

Writers of fiction sometimes describe the characters they have created as taking on a life of their own. Even though these characters come from the author's imagination, it is as if they can resist the author's control. Writers sometimes describe themselves as discovering how their characters will respond in particular situations, rather than simply deciding what they will do. Sometimes they even report being surprised at what their characters do or finding that the characters won't behave in ways that are needed for plot purposes. In other words, writing a novel sometimes feels like creating something that has a kind of independence from the creator that should be respected.

Suppose we think of God as composing the story of the universe. One way to imagine the composition is to think of it as formed in all its details in God's mind and then acted out just as God envisions. God, we might say, won't be surprised at anything because it is all part of the plan. But what if we imagine a different kind of composition, one where the characters really do have their own points of view and their own capacity for independent action? Instead of thinking that God's characters are limited to a script, imagine that they are given the opportunity to improvise.[3] Of course, their improvisation will depend on the natures and potentials they have been given, but those natures may include a capacity for creative action that is not just pre-programmed.

What I am calling the characters will, of course, include human agents who make choices. But I am also including in the cast of characters physical systems that act in orderly, but not entirely predictable ways.[4] We might think of God as setting up the fundamental parameters that define the nature of physical systems, but then allowing things to operate in accordance with the powers and potentials they have been given.

To create something finite with the capacity for genuine independence, God needs to establish a sphere of existence in which the powers of finite things produce actual results. But if God's control can't be limited by anything else, any appearance of finite control would be an illusion. There is a strain of Jewish thought that portrays creation as a kind of withdrawal through which God makes room for the existence of something other than God.[5] On this understanding, the realm in which we exist comes about through an act of divine limitation. If the existence of creatures like us depends on God pulling back from control so that there is room for us, then we might think of such a withdrawal by God as an act of love.

Conceiving of God as creating beings with their own capacity for autonomous action and their own sphere of control makes it easier to understand why God's will is not always done in our world. Created things with

---

3. Polkinghorne, "Kenotic Creation," 94.

4. Our best science tells us that what we call the laws of nature are probabilistic rather than deterministic.

5. Isaac Luria uses the term *"tzimtzum"* (which can be translated as withdrawal). See Scholem, *Major Trends*, 260–61.

a capacity for independence are potential sources of outcomes that are in opposition to God's intentions. It might seem paradoxical that God could make something that could resist divine intentions. But it is paradoxical only if we cannot conceive of God as letting go of power in relation to finite things. Physicist and theologian John Polkinghorne applies the biblical term *kenosis* (self-emptying)[6] to God's creative activity. He says, "The act of creation involves divine acceptance of the risk of the existence of the other, and there is a consequent *kenosis* of God's omnipotence. This curtailment of divine power . . . arises from the logic of love, which requires the freedom of the beloved."[7]

In creating a universe where finite beings will to a significant extent determine what happens, God accepts that evils will occur in that universe. However, creating a universe that will give rise to evils is different from intending any particular evil. If your son dies before the age of two because of a genetic disease, you can say that God created a universe in which diseases like this can happen, but not that God decided that your son die at that time. If your best friend betrays you, you can say that the betrayal was made possible by a universe in which people can act in this way, but not that God wanted it to happen. There will be evils such as these in a universe where physical regularities and free choice determine much of what happens, but if creation involves giving up control, it is seriously misleading to think of each evil as ordained by God.

To use an analogy, suppose you are designing the highway system in your state.[8] You might be able to predict that some number of serious accidents are likely to occur. But that does not mean in designing the system you want any of them to occur, and it certainly does not mean when on November 22 of some year a young mother is struck and killed by a drunk driver, you decided that it would happen. The highway system you designed may have made the event possible, but this awful event was not something you were seeking, and its occurrence was beyond your control.

But are the awful things that happen in the universe beyond God's control? Some people would suggest that even if creaturely freedom plays a role in how things go, God knows how finite creatures will act and incorporates that information into the script. So, in creating, God is still choosing each thing that happens in the world. However, the alternative that I am suggesting involves not just what Polkinghorne calls a "curtailment of divine power," but also a curtailment of divine knowledge. I agree with

---

6. The term is used in Phil 2 to describe Christ giving up divine prerogatives.
7. Polkinghorne, *Faith of a Physicist*, 81.
8. Hasker, *Triumph of God*, 205.

philosophers called *open theists* who say that when God makes a temporal universe with a genuinely open future, even God cannot fully know everything that will happen. I won't argue for that view here, but others have made a persuasive case for it.[9]

BUT WHAT ABOUT MIRACLES?

Some people would reject the claim that God is not in control of everything that happens in the world by suggesting that God can always do something miraculous. Piper's claim that God could use a wind to blow the 9/11 planes away seems to involve such an idea. However, thinking of miracles as a way of maintaining control over what happens means imagining that God alters the consequences of human choices or natural processes on a regular basis. It presumes something like the image of God acting as a micromanager who determines in each situation whether to allow things to proceed or to change the natural course of events. This picture, however, conflicts with the idea that God's relation to the created world involves a kind of withdrawal that allows created beings to develop in their own way. If God continually hovers over us to correct things that might otherwise go wrong, there is not all that much room for created beings to have genuine independence.

There is another problem with the idea that God can override the natural order at any point to achieve results that are more desirable. What we observe gives us reason to think that people are usually allowed to suffer from events such as earthquakes, tsunamis, diseases, car crashes, and acts of human violence. If acting to prevent such tragedies is always an option, why doesn't God do more to prevent terrible suffering? The greater you imagine God's power to step in and alter the natural course of events, the more difficult it is to answer that question.

It might be thought that my talk of divine withdrawal amounts to a deistic view of things, i.e., thinking that God creates the universe, but does not act in it. However, the kind of withdrawal needed for independence of the created order does not imply that God can do nothing in the world. There is a range of alternatives between God acting as a micromanager of everything and God having no involvement in what happens. We may find, however, that our thinking about the alternatives is hampered by a commonly accepted picture of God's options. We tend to imagine that God must either let things take their natural course or intervene from outside the natural order and that the decision of which to do is totally up to God.

---

9. See for example, Hasker, *God, Time, and Knowledge*; Pinnock, *Openness of God*; Swinburne, *Coherence of Theism*.

The dominant biblical picture of God's relation to the world suggests a different way of conceiving things. Ancient Hebrews thought that there were particular places in the world where God was especially present. The temple was the prime example. Heaven (God's realm) and earth were thought of as united at this location. So, instead of imagining God as outside our realm and sometimes intervening to do a miracle, we might take a hint from the biblical picture and think of God's reality as overlapping or interlacing earthly reality.[10] In one sense God's presence is everywhere, but it may be manifest to a higher degree at times and places where there is a kind of harmony between heavenly and earthly reality. We could think of such a harmony as making possible some events that do not conform to our standard expectations of how the world operates. However, thinking in these terms suggests that what God can do in the world may depend to some extent on the receptiveness of created things to the divine presence. To put it another way, there may need to be the right kind of vessels through which divine power can flow.

There is a suggestion in the gospels that what God can do through Jesus depends to a significant extent on human responsiveness. Jesus says frequently to those who are healed, "Your faith has saved you." "Faith" here seems to mean something like receptiveness to God. So, we might understand Jesus's words to mean that displays of the power of God depend on willing recipients of what God seeks to do. Recall also the statement in the Gospels that when Jesus went to Nazareth, "he could do no deed of power there, because of their unbelief" (Matt 13:58). This text suggests that what God is able to do can be blocked by human resistance.

So, when we ask whether God can perform some miraculous act, such as blowing away the 9/11 planes, perhaps we should be cautious in our confident assumptions about what God can do. Keith Ward notes that the term "miracle" is most often used in connection with "the extraordinary deeds and events that surround the lives of prophets, teachers, and saints . . ."[11] Perhaps we can posit that the occurrence of miracles involves "persons who are unusually attuned to the divine mind" becoming mediators through whom God's power can accomplish extraordinary things.[12] If we think of miracles in this way, we can accept the possibility of remarkable manifestations of divine power, though we should refrain from assuming that whatever we can imagine in a given situation is something God can do,

---

10. Wright, *Simply Christian*, 60–66.
11. Ward, *Pascal's Fire*, 222.
12. Ward, *Pascal's Fire*, 222.

since we are typically ignorant of what conditions might be needed to make an extraordinary event possible.

GOD'S POWER AND THE CROSS

Many people have difficulty thinking that God's power to do things might depend on human cooperation. Real power, they think, can simply overcome any opposition. Perhaps, however, we should recall that the central Christian image for God's redemptive power is the cross. This image can easily suggest to us weakness rather than strength, but Paul says that his message of Christ crucified is "the power of God and the wisdom of God." (1 Cor 1:24). In contrast to the classic hero who goes into battle with weapons of war to fight against and conquer the enemy, Jesus refuses to meet force with force, enduring the aggressive actions of those who oppose him without responding in kind. Instead of a display of overwhelming strength that subdues any opposition, we find instead a steadfast refusal to play the human power game.

The kind of vulnerability and restraint we see in the cross resembles the laying down of power I have posited in relation to creation. In each case we might say that God's vulnerability and restraint exhibit what Polkinghorne calls "the logic of love." In creation God lets go of control to give created powers room to develop in their own way, accepting how they shape the world even when it conflicts with God wants for the created order, and in the cross God continues to allow created beings to have their way even when people violently oppose Jesus's proclamation of God's kingdom.

If we accept the idea that God gives us the space to pursue our own way, even when it leads to despicable outcomes, it might seem that evil is given free rein. Yet amazingly, Christians have understood the cross to represent a triumph over evil. The triumph they describe does not seem to be a matter of stopping evildoers in their tracks. It is rather that Christians see in Jesus one in whom the powers that fuel evil are replaced by the greater power of self-giving love. Moreover, the New Testament witness is that the spread of the kind of love revealed in Jesus will ultimately mean the undoing of power structures that distort God's intentions for human life.

I will say more in subsequent chapters about the New Testament vision of how evil is to be overcome. But here I want to address briefly what it means at an individual level to think that God is not controlling everything that happens.

A RISKY WORLD

We live in a risky world, a world in which terrible things can happen to you and to those you love. Hardly anyone avoids significant loss. It is worth noticing that thinking that God controls everything does not make the world any less risky. All the bad things that happen still occur whether you believe that God is arranging them or not, and even if you think everything happens for a reason, you are likely to find many things for which you can discover no reasons that really satisfy you.

My rejection of the claim that everything happens for a reason is not a rejection of the claim that sometimes God uses particular things that happen to bring about some good purpose. In Genesis Joseph says to his brothers who sold him into slavery, "Even though you intended to do me harm, God intended it for good, in order to preserve a numerous people as he is doing today" (Gen 50:20). I don't think that the point here is that God intended all along that Joseph's brothers sell him into slavery or that his going into slavery was somehow fated. It is rather that when bad things happen, God can sometimes use them to bring about something good. Even if it is not true that everything happens for a reason, there are sometimes patterns that reveal a larger purpose.

Sometimes we see signs of what God is doing in the world. However, we need to be cautious about our interpretations. It may seem as if God saved your family from dying in a train wreck, but when you look at those in the next car who didn't make it, do you think that God singled out your family for survival and didn't show mercy on others? Don't be too sure. Not every good thing is the result of some special act of God. Some good results come about from being lucky enough to have good genes or good instruction or being in the right place at the right time. You can be thankful for the good things that happen in your life without thinking that you are one of God's special favorites who gets protection that others do not. You can be attentive to what God may be doing in your life, without concluding that God arranged it whenever you have good fortune or that God is punishing you whenever you have bad fortune.

Acknowledging that God does not control everything that happens can be disturbing, but it can also be liberating. You can admit what seems obvious: that not everything turns out for the best, instead of grasping for bogus explanations. You can be honest about hating some things that happen, without thinking that you are questioning God's plan. You can also sympathize with others who are suffering, without worrying that God wants them to suffer.

Recognizing that there are forces in the world that constrain what God can do is also helpful in understanding the phenomenon of unanswered prayer. A common response to why requests are not granted is to claim that God sometimes says no or says to wait. However, it is puzzling to think that God is able to give people what they request, but sometimes refrains from doing so, even when the request is clearly for something that is in accordance with what God wants for the world. I think that the problem here is connected with imagining petitionary prayer as involving something like requests to a celestial switchboard in which God receives requests and unilaterally decides to grant some and reject others. It might be better to reverse the order and to think of God as wanting to do things in the world, but potentially being blocked by lack of human cooperation. Our prayers may sometimes enable God to act by serving as expressions of our willingness to cooperate with God's purposes. Some things, however, are not just up to us individually. We may be praying for things that are blocked by lack of cooperation from other people or by resistance from systems that perpetuate oppression and violence. Thinking in such terms may help us to understand the biblical injunction to persistent prayer.[13]

When awful and senseless things happen, what may help more than facile explanations of why a particular thing happened is remembering that the Christian revelation is not of a God who sits aloof with folded arms in a distant place. It is instead of one who has come among us, one who shares our suffering and understands what we're going through (Heb 4:15). It is counterproductive to pretend that everything that happens to you is good, but you can affirm that in everything God is seeking your good, which is ultimately to become like Christ (Rom 8:29). And rather than despairing that what you do doesn't matter, you can recognize with amazement that you may become one of the willing human vessels through whom God's power to transform things can be activated.

---

13. Wink, *Powers That Be*, 187–98.

CHAPTER 13

Signs and Wonders

ED WILKINSON, A MEMBER of a Christian church in the United States, had a background in neuropsychology that predisposed him to skepticism about claims of miraculous events. He didn't deny the possibility, but he thought people too often sought supernatural help instead of "dealing with reality." His ideas faced a challenge when his eight-year-old son Brad was diagnosed with an atrial septal defect. There were two holes in the boy's heart, and his activities were severely limited while he awaited major surgery. During the lengthy waiting period, Brad apparently recognized the seriousness of his condition. He started giving away his toys in the expectation that he would not survive. Brad asked his father directly one day if he was going to die, and his father acknowledged that he might. Brad then asked, "Can Jesus heal me?" Not knowing what to say, Ed replied, "I'll get back to you on that." A few days later, after some anguished prayer, Ed told his son that God does heal, but that even if healing did not happen, there was still the promise of eternal life.

During a church service a visiting minister called for those who needed healing to come forward. At Ed's urging, Brad went to the minister and explained his problem. The minister offered a simple prayer for Brad's healing. Medical tests the next week showed that Brad's condition was unchanged. The next day he was taken to surgery, which was expected to last four to six hours. After an hour, the surgeon came to the waiting room. He explained that on the image viewed as the operation was about to begin, the places where blood had been leaking from one chamber of the heart to another could not be detected. He assured Ed that there had been no misdiagnosis.

The holes in the heart that had been there the previous day had gone away. The surgeon suggested that someone must have been praying.[1]

This example of extraordinary healing is not unique. There are numerous accounts from countries all over the world of healings that defy ordinary expectations. Reports of this kind come both from our own time and from other historical periods where we have records. Many of the accounts are even more dramatic than the example I cite. They include stories of blind people instantly receiving sight, lame people walking, malignant tumors disappearing, and much more.[2] In our era people who have been influenced by Western education have a higher level of skepticism about such accounts than people in most cultures today and all cultures prior to the Enlightenment. Our thinking about such matters is connected with our acceptance of science, but it is not science alone that leads us to dismiss or minimize the significance of claims about extraordinary events, even when they are backed by strong testimonial support. Our confidence in science becomes entangled with a worldview that accepts as real only what fits with scientific explanations of what happens in the world.

The worldview I am referring to can be called *scientific naturalism*. Naturalism says that nothing exists other than nature. Hence, it rejects influences on nature by anything beyond the natural realm. But the version of naturalism I am calling a worldview says something more. It says that the understanding of how nature works found in contemporary science marks the limits of what can occur. Given this approach, if there are reports of phenomena that don't fit with our current scientific understanding, the scientific naturalist will conclude that the reports are untrue. This kind of skepticism about extraordinary events is not itself a scientific conclusion. Science has no way to verify the claim that whatever happens is explainable in terms of contemporary scientific views of how nature operates. But even people with beliefs that conflict with the claims of scientific naturalism can find that this worldview influences how they think.

When Ed Wilkinson tells his son that God can heal, he is presumably acknowledging that something beyond the natural order can affect what happens. So, he is not a scientific naturalist. But his skepticism about claims of divine action suggests that for practical purposes, he assumes the world can be understood in terms of the kinds of regularities scientists describe. Even if there are rare exceptions, he can mostly disregard them as not relevant to thinking about what to expect. In other words, scientific naturalism

---

1. Keener, *Miracles*, 1, 432–33.
2. For an extensive account see Keener's two-volume study, *Miracles*.

functions for him as a default position, which might be overridden, but generally guides his thinking.

Ed thinks of the approach that makes him skeptical of claims about extraordinary events that defy scientific understanding as "dealing with reality." Admittedly, it is often sensible to accept what seems likely, given the way nature works. Having faith that my stage 3 cancer will go away can be a form of denial. However, even if relying on a scientific understanding of nature is useful for predicting what typically happens, adopting scientific naturalism as a default position for thinking about the world carries with it the risk that we will slip into thinking of it as a reliable test of what is real. When we presume the truth of scientific naturalism, other ways of understanding reality tend to fade from view. It becomes easy to miss or reject signs that might point to something beyond the natural order. We are also less likely to recognize regularities that are entirely natural, but not explainable in terms of the kind of scientific theorizing we regard as well-established.

Ed is representative of a great many people who accept Christian teachings, but have difficulty integrating them with a habitual way of thinking about the world as a material order that operates in predictable ways. One way that some Christians deal with the tension is to affirm the existence of a Creator, but think of God as distant and uninvolved with the world. A variant of this view holds that God acted in the world in biblical times, but no longer does so. These lines of thought seem to me to be recipes for a very thin form of Christian faith that gives up the idea that God makes a real difference in how things go. Furthermore, when the underlying presumption that science can explain what happens in the world is combined with a view that scientifically minded people often find attractive—that the only reliable way to know about reality is through sense experience—little room is left for something that seems fundamental to having a religious outlook: a *sense of mystery*. Finding the world to be a place of mystery, as I am using the term, depends on a kind of openness to events or experiences that may alert us to dimensions of reality that transcend the "world of ordinary everyday life."[3]

All of the major world religions speak of a deeper level of reality than the world we encounter through ordinary sensory experience. The worldviews that were accepted by most people prior to the rise of scientific naturalism made room for contact with this deeper reality through means other than the senses. It was assumed that people might encounter the sacred through such experiences as dreams or visions or ecstatic states during which the veil hiding the deeper reality was lowered.

---

3. Berger, *Questions of Faith*, 102.

In Western cultures there is a tendency to dismiss claims that these kinds of experiences tell us anything about reality. We tend to think that moving away from the kind of perception we have in ordinary waking states means going into the realm of subjectivity or fantasy. This way of thinking is connected with regarding science as the measure of what is objectively real. If science tells us what is really there, then experiences suggesting a deeper level of reality than science discovers have to be downgraded. When we do so, however, we are cutting ourselves off from vital sources of biblical faith: experiences involving conscious states that differ from ordinary conscious awareness.

ALTERED STATES OF CONSCIOUSNESS

It is well known that different animals have different ways of perceiving the world. For example, bats have a way of interacting with the environment we do not possess. They locate objects such as insects by receiving the echoes of ultrasonic sounds the bats emit. Even when we do have a comparable type of sense experience, members of a different species may pick up what we don't detect. Think, for example, of birds that can see much farther than a human being or dogs whose sense of smell surpasses ours. What we hear or see is not everything that might be heard or seen, but only a select range on the spectrum of light waves and sound waves. There are presumably explanations of how the kinds of perceptual abilities we possess have developed because of their survival value for our species in the physical environment we inhabit. But my point is that we have reason to think that our senses connect us with reality in a very selective way.

There is also reason to suspect that the kind of conscious experience that makes us aware of sensations involves a type of selection that cuts us off from information that we possess at an unconscious level. Philosophers such as Henri Bergson and C. D. Broad have developed the idea that what we call ordinary consciousness arises as a survival mechanism to keep us from being flooded with data that would hamper our ability to act effectively in the physical environment. On their accounts the brain functions as a kind of filtering or reducing valve that screens out a great deal of non-sensory input, blocking us most of the time from a kind of contact with reality that does not make it into conscious awareness.

Our access to a wider range of inputs depends on what we can call *altered states of consciousness*. The American philosopher William James writes, " . . . our normal waking consciousness, rational consciousness as we call it, is but one special type of consciousness, whilst all about it, parted from it by the filmiest of screens, there lie potential forms of consciousness entirely different."[4] Altered states can be produced by such means as drugs or meditative practices, but they can also occur spontaneously. Such states include dreams and waking visions, as well as trance states, including hypnotic trances. They also include various types of mystical states that purport to give individuals direct contact with something transcending the physical order. In altered states the operation of filters that usually restrict the information we receive is relaxed, and we become aware of some of what is usually blocked by the kind of consciousness that accompanies ordinary sense experience.

The disputable issue is what our awareness in these altered states tells us about reality. People who have mystical experiences typically claim that these experiences can put us in touch with a level of reality that is more fundamental than what we encounter through ordinary sense experience. As the poet W. H. Auden puts it, when after a mystical experience someone "... returns to a normal state, he does not say: 'That was a pleasant dream, but, of course, an illusion. Now I am awake and see things as they really are'; he says 'For a moment the veil was lifted and I saw what really is.'"[5]

Consider a description of a mystical experience William James quotes in a classic work on religious experience:

> I remember the night, and almost the very spot on the hilltop, where my soul opened out, as it were to the Infinite, and there was a rushing together of two worlds, the inner and the outer. . . . I stood alone with Him who had made me, and all the beauty of the world, and love, and sorrow, and even temptation. . . . The ordinary sense of things around me faded . . . I could not any more have doubted that *He* was there than that I was. Indeed, I felt myself to be, if possible, the less real of the two.[6]

I quote this account, not to prove the reality of God. I suspect that the way people describe their mystical encounters is greatly affected by beliefs they already have. In this case we have a description by a Christian minister. I am citing the account as an example of a fairly full-blown description of a mystical encounter in which ordinary perceptual awareness fades away and an awareness emerges of what seems to the person to be a deeper level of reality. That kind of assessment is typical of how mystics describe their experiences.

---

4. James, *Varieties*, 298.
5. Auden, "Introduction," 8.
6. James, *Varieties*, 67.

Of course, the fact that mystics think that they are encountering reality at a more fundamental level does not prove that they are correct. But it does put the dispute between scientific naturalism and alternative worldviews in a different light. After studying these kinds of experiences at length, James concludes that "the existence of mystical states absolutely overthrows the pretension of non-mystical states to be the sole ultimate dictators of what we may believe."[7] In other words, the existence of these states means that a description of reality based only on the way things seem to us in our ordinary waking consciousness depends on an assumption that can be questioned. James thinks it is an "open question whether mystical states may not possibly be . . . superior points of view, windows through which the mind looks out on a more extensive and inclusive world."[8] Accepting such a wider reality can alter the way we asses some events that don't seem to make sense from the point of view of scientific naturalism. What might seem impossible from that viewpoint could be a manifestation of the "more extensive and inclusive world" that is ordinarily hidden from us.

MIRACLES?

You can obviously be too credulous about accounts of extraordinary events. But how skeptical should you be? If you accept scientific naturalism, you can acknowledge surprising events that come about through such things as coincidences or spontaneous remissions. But you will have to draw the line at what you think can't happen because of the way you understand the natural order to operate. With regard to some claims, no amount of evidence could be enough. William James reports that some of his scientific colleagues at Harvard were unwilling to investigate claims to telepathic awareness for which he found credible evidence. They simply ruled out in advance the idea that this sort of thing could happen because it did not fit with their scientific understanding of how the world works.

Some worldviews allow for a greater degree of openness to the extraordinary. If we think that there is a deeper level of reality than the physical order, we can posit that it may sometimes show itself in ways that are unexpected from the scientific point of view. It all depends, of course, on how the deeper level is conceived. But someone who thinks that there is more to reality than science discloses may make different judgments about what claims are plausible than the scientific naturalist, leading to different

---

7. James, *Varieties*, 327.
8. James, *Varieties*, 327.

assessments of what evidence is needed to accept reports about events that are unexpected from the scientific viewpoint.

Are we talking about miracles? To meaningfully answer yes or no, we need to have some agreement about what the term "miracle" means. Some people use the term so broadly that any event that produces a sense of awe is called a miracle. For example, I have heard people say that the birth of a baby is a miracle, even though birth is clearly a recurring part of the natural order. At the opposite extreme are those who say that a miracle has to involve some kind of violation of natural law. They hold that only events that cannot have occurred through ordinary natural processes can be considered miraculous. It is in this sense of the term that David Hume famously argued in the eighteenth century that you should never believe a miracle story.[9]

It is important to notice that biblical writers did not speak of extraordinary events as violations of laws of nature for the simple reason that they did not have our concept of a law of nature. They could, of course, recognize the difference between the kind of event that can be expected in the normal course of things and events that conflict with standard expectations. The most common way to translate terms they used for the latter kind of event is as signs or wonders. Such terms were used to refer to extraordinary events that manifest divine power or in some cases powers other than God, such as the wonders produced by the Egyptian magicians in Exod 7–8 or the works of false prophets referred to in Matt 24.

So, if by "miracle" we mean a sign or wonder in the biblical sense, we are talking about an event that goes against what we would ordinarily expect apart from the operation of some kind of extraordinary power. An advantage to framing the issue in terms of expectations rather than in terms of violations of natural law is that it can be very difficult to figure out in a given case whether an occurrence should be thought of as violating a law of nature. Think, for example, of the healing story at the beginning of this chapter. We can recognize in this case and others that a particular healing is very unlikely. But for all we know, it may be a surprising example of natural events that sometimes happen. Some might object that if we don't know a natural law has been violated, we cannot be sure that divine action is involved. But the point of biblical signs and wonders is not really to provide that kind of proof. It is to serve as pointers to divine action for those who are receptive enough to recognize it. God can presumably achieve this function through events that don't involve any violation of natural law.

Some people would say that regardless of how we think of miracles in relation to the natural order, the Creator of nature could always override

---

9. Hume, *Inquiry*, 96–116.

nature's operations at will. I have given reasons in the last chapter for being cautious in claiming to know exactly what kind of control God has. In particular I have rejected the view that God can do whatever we can imagine. But I don't reject claims that some pretty remarkable things can happen in the world, including some things that are inexplicable from the point of view of our scientific understanding of how the world works. Further, I think that some credible reports of extraordinary events give us reason to think that scientific naturalism is an inadequate way to think about reality.[10]

UNEXPECTED POWERS

Miracles are often understood as interventions into the natural order by a higher power that overrules that order. But consider another way to conceive them. What if extraordinary events that conflict with our expectations are manifestations of a deeper level of the natural order through which human beings are enabled to exercise powers that are not normally under their control? Instead of thinking that God occasionally overrides some natural regularity, we might think of such events as coming about when unexpected powers that we possess potentially are activated.

I am going to focus first on an unexpected power that I think is closely associated with extraordinary cases of healing: the power to make changes in our own bodies that we can't do by conscious effort. The existence of what is called the placebo effect is not open to serious dispute, but the results of its operation can sometimes seem incredible. The placebo effect involves powers to heal the body that are activated when someone is in the right kind of mental state. This effect comes about when people who are suffering from some malady become convinced that something has been done that will make them better. Typically, someone else's action is involved, such as a physician who does something that stimulates a patient's mind in a way that activates healing processes.

We can get some idea of how this power operates by noting the similarity between the placebo effect and instances of posthypnotic suggestion. A person can be told under hypnosis to make the body do something that people can't do by intentional effort, such as forming a blister on the skin or eliminating the pain response to what is ordinarily painful. The hypnotic suggestion apparently activates powers of mind that exist at an unconscious level. The placebo effect seems to involve a similar kind of response to suggestion that is received by the unconscious mind.

10. For others who draw this conclusion, see Braude, *Crimes of Reason* and Grosso, *Smile of the Universe*.

A common misunderstanding of the placebo effect involves thinking that it applies only in cases of psychosomatic illness, i.e., illness that is produced or exacerbated by mental factors. In fact, the placebo effect can occur regardless of the cause of someone's condition. Some instances of cancers that are apparently incurable, but go away, should probably be understood in terms of the activation of unconscious powers of the mind to heal the body. How far such powers extend is hard to say, but we can get some idea by attending to credible accounts of unexpected cures of a very wide range of diseases and disabilities.

We might speculate that people who exhibit abilities to heal others by nonmedical means make use of the placebo effect by acting in ways that stimulate the right kinds of mental states in the person suffering from some problem. One healer I read about, who over a number of years achieved remarkable results, made extensive use of mental imagery in praying for the patient to let go of harmful emotions and replace them with more positive attitudes and emotions.[11] We might surmise that hearing prayers of this kind sometimes activates unconscious processes in the one prayed for that contribute to healing.

Even so, it seems remarkable that the unconscious mind is able to unlock these healing powers. This phenomenon is reminiscent of reported cases in which the unconscious mind enables someone to perform complex calculations or play musical instruments or communicate in a foreign language without learning to do any of these things. Sometimes striking abilities even occur in people who are intellectually disabled (savant syndrome). Somehow people are able to tap into unconscious knowledge and skills that surpass what they know or can do at a conscious level. We can say these phenomena show the mind to have hidden depths, but there is surely cause to wonder about what kind of reality could give rise to the kinds of knowledge and skills displayed. It is tempting to suspect that the individual mind may be connected with some larger whole through which unexpected knowledge or skills become available. The temptation is magnified when we consider a wider range of powers that appear to be connected with the unconscious mind.

EXPANDED AWARENESS AND INFLUENCE

We exist as physical beings in a world of physical things. But we are also beings who have minds, and there is good reason to think that these minds sometimes do things that standard scientific accounts cannot explain.

11. Sanford, *Healing Gifts*.

Sometimes people become aware of what they could not be aware of through ordinary perception. In other words, they display what has been called extrasensory perception. Similarly, sometimes our minds produce physical effects that go beyond the kind of power we have to affect our own bodies. This sort of influence is usually called psychokinesis. The claim that such powers exist is widely disputed, but I am convinced that it is supported both by cross-cultural reports from many time periods, including our own, as well as extensive laboratory testing that has produced strong statistical evidence.[12] I suspect that resistance to recognizing the force of the available evidence is generally a result of not studying it or of looking at it from the perspective of a worldview that rules these phenomena out as impossible.

These powers seem to be connected to capacities of the unconscious mind. Experiments show much greater levels of extrasensory perception by people in altered states of consciousness, such as dream states or in states produced by sensory deprivation, where the restraints of ordinary consciousness are relaxed.[13] Meditative traditions contain numerous reports of striking abilities displayed by those who achieve particular altered states through meditation.[14] In Christian tradition paranormal attainments accompanying meditation are sometimes called *charisms*. In Hindu tradition they are called *siddhis*. The Indian thinker Patanjali connects *siddhis* with a state he calls *samyama*, which involves a kind of concentration in which the sense of self recedes and one becomes absorbed in the image or activity concentrated on. Reports of *siddhis* include such things as extraordinary knowledge, extraordinary strength, unusual control over bodily processes, and even levitation.

Some people doubt the existence of psychic powers on the grounds that people cannot do such things on demand. I think that there is a plausible explanation why. Ordinary waking consciousness and the reflection that goes with it overwhelms the unconscious sources of this kind of power. One way to think about the various meditative traditions is that they provide techniques for reducing the mental noise that accompanies what we think of as ordinary consciousness. Some people are more skilled or have greater natural abilities in this area than others, though there is evidence of some level of psychic ability across the general population. One interesting

---

12. For a sample of scholars who are convinced of the reality of psychic phenomena, see Kelly, *Irreducible Mind*; Griffin, *Parapsychology, Philosophy, and Spirituality*; and Braude, *ESP and Psychokinesis*. For an overview of laboratory evidence see Radin, *Conscious Universe*.

13. Michael Schmicker, *Best Evidence*, 67, 70–73.

14. Radin, *Supernormal*.

experimental result is that people who believe in such powers are more likely than those who do not to give evidence of them.

But how can connecting with the unconscious give rise to unusual powers? If we listen to the testimony of mystics, we learn of widespread experiences that suggest the inadequacy of the way we typically think of ourselves. In the ordinary state of consciousness, the mind is experienced as an isolated entity, separate from other minds and from the physical environment. But mystics often report a dissolving of this sense of separateness. Some of them interpret their experience to mean that there is no individual self. A less radical interpretation is that at a deep level the mind is connected with a wider reality that for lack of a better term we can call a spiritual dimension. We could posit that it is by means of such a connection that we gain access to knowledge and skills that we don't ordinarily have.

Philosopher John Hick interprets the data of psychical research and mystical experience to support the view that our minds are linked to other minds in such a way that what happens in one mind affects other minds. He offers the following account of why prayer for others is sometimes effective:

> We are all linked at a deep unconscious level in a universal network, in which our thoughts, and even more our emotions, are all the time affecting others, as others are in turn affecting us. When in prayer or meditation, we direct our thoughts to a particular individual, this is intensified. . . . In the case of bodily healing, another's mind affects the patient's mind, which in turn affects the patient's body.[15]

What Hick posits here is something that should not occur if we think of reality in purely physical terms, but which seems possible if we think that there is a spiritual dimension of reality through which such links occur.[16]

If there are powers of mind that humans possess that may lead to the occurrence of things we regard as extraordinary, then extraordinary events are not necessarily specific acts of God. Just as much of what happens in the world is the product of what we might think of as ordinary powers God builds into the created order, some events may be the result of additional powers that are activated when human capacities that are developed in the right way or when the right conditions are realized. Nevertheless, there is nothing in this account that precludes the possibility that God sometimes uses unexpected powers of mind to produce extraordinary events. In fact, if we posit that human beings can influence other people's minds in the way

---

15. Hick, *Fifth Dimension*, 19.

16. For attempts to come to terms with a reality in which psychic phenomena are real, see Kelly, *Beyond Physicalism*; Taylor, *Spiritual Science;* and Tart, *End of Materialism*.

that Hick suggests, it doesn't seem strange at all that the divine Mind could influence us. Some of these influences might lead to events that strike us as miraculous, but others might seem hardly noticeable.

The idea that God could work through the unconscious mind to activate latent human powers seems to me to fit with my earlier claims that God's method of working in the world involves human cooperation. If God reveals something to the unconscious mind or urges someone to act by means of an unconscious impulse, it is likely the kind of influence we can resist. On the other hand, if we are receptive to what God does, we may become channels for divine action. Being a channel for God's action does not have to mean doing something miraculous. But when people have significant psychic potentials and are also well attuned to God's purposes, signs and wonders may occur. I think that in Jesus these conditions were fulfilled in the highest degree. He had the kind of connection to the spiritual order that made possible extraordinary acts that served God's revelatory and redemptive purposes.

To be clear, I am not saying we should believe all miracle stories, either those we hear about in the present day or those we read in the Bible. Critical judgment is entirely appropriate. But I do want to suggest that we have good reason to think there is a depth to reality that our scientific accounts do not capture and that recognizing this depth can help us overcome the spell of a worldview that restricts our ability to think of God doing anything in the world. If we can learn to take off the blinders, we may be better able to recognize the signs of God's activity and become more receptive to the prospect of experiential contact with God.

PART 4

Substantive Faith

CHAPTER 14

God's New Order
Welcome News for the Excluded

I GREW UP IN a church tradition that taught me to think the central gospel message was about being saved so I could go to heaven when I died. When I read the Bible, I understood what it said in the light of what I had been trained to expect. I tended not to notice if biblical texts said things that did not fit with this way of understanding the message because I had learned to read these texts in ways that made them seem to fit. For example, when passages from the Gospels referred to entering the kingdom of God (or the kingdom of heaven), I understood them to be about going to heaven. Jesus, I assumed, must be focused on preparing people for the next life.

Only after learning to look at these texts with fresh eyes did it become apparent to me that I had misunderstood them. The focus of Jesus's message was not on what would happen after death, but on a work of God that he said was already beginning to happen during his ministry. What he announced was not an escape to heaven, but "God's sovereign rule coming 'on earth as it is in heaven.'"[1] To those receiving his message, Jesus offered the opportunity to participate in a new order through which God's will for human life on earth would finally be fulfilled.

Part of what blocked me from recognizing such a message were teachings I had received that led me to think of the world as a lost cause. At some point, presumably very soon, God was going to intervene to call a halt to the world and take the faithful to heaven. Things on earth, I was told, would not get any better before the end came. There was no hope for real improvement

1. Wright, *Surprised By Hope*, 18.

in the world, only the hope of leaving earthly existence behind. Of course, good works should be done in the meantime, including meeting people's physical needs. But the most important concern was meeting people's spiritual needs by helping them make sure of their eternal destiny. If the Bible contained teachings about God's intention to transform life on earth, I was programmed not to recognize them.

THE KINGDOM OF GOD

Biblical scholars agree that the central topic of Jesus's teaching was what Mark and Luke call the kingdom of God. Matthew, writing primarily to a Jewish audience, substitutes the phrase "kingdom of heaven." It is usually thought that the substitution is because of Jewish sensibilities about pronouncing the divine name. But whatever the reason for the difference, it is clear that these two terms refer to the same reality.

The phrase "kingdom of God" connects with Israel's understanding of her past and her hopes for the future. The Jewish people had been ruled by kings until the time of the Babylonian conquest. However, the ideal for the nation was for the king to serve as a human representative who would facilitate God's rule. It had never quite worked out that way. In biblical histories most of the kings are condemned for failing to lead the nation in accordance with God's commands, especially the command not to worship other gods. Even the kings who avoided the worst failings were typically more caught up in personal agendas than in fulfilling Israel's unique vocation as a people of God. Nevertheless, there arises a persistent expectation in the prophetic writings that one day God will send a king (a Messiah) who will put things right. In Jesus's day most Jews understood this expectation to mean restoring national independence and power, as well as some kind of judgment on foreign nations. Jesus announces at the beginning of his ministry that the time for God's deliverance has arrived. But his vision of what God will do through him does not line up with what people were expecting of the Messiah.

In the temptation story told in Matthew and Luke, Jesus is portrayed as wrestling with alternative ways of being the Messiah that fit with widespread expectations of the time. One is to use the way of force to build an empire. He can have authority over all the kingdoms of the world, but the price is to accept the violent methods of control that earthly kingdoms have always been built on. We could say that the temptation is to accomplish good through evil means. It is tempting to think that if you had control, you could accomplish many great things. Jesus could no doubt imagine the harm he might prevent to the weak and vulnerable. But gaining and retaining control means dealing with whatever opposition stands in the way by the brutal methods characteristic of earthly kingdoms. Jews expected that the Messiah would use military power as earthly kings always did, but when it came time to declare himself, Jesus enters Jerusalem, not on a war horse but on a donkey. He comes on a mission of peace, rather than a mission of violent rebellion against foreign rule (Mark 11:1–8; Matt 21:1–5).

In the Gospel of John Jesus is described as telling Pilate that his kingdom is not from this world (John 18:36). This claim is sometimes taken to mean that it is a kingdom that deals with other-worldly concerns rather than life here and now, so Pilate can rest assured that Jesus is no threat to earthly kingdoms. But this interpretation is mistaken. While Jesus in this account is contrasting his kingdom with kingdoms that have an earthly origin, he is not claiming that his kingdom is about life in some other realm rather than life on earth. Nor is he denying that his kingdom will pose a challenge for earthly kingdoms. True enough, he is not raising an army or authorizing a violent uprising to overthrow the powers that be. But he is unleashing a kind of power that in due course can undermine claims to authority of kingdoms that have earthly origins. The early Christians understood that when they proclaimed Jesus as Lord, they were rejecting the claim that Caesar is Lord. They were pledging their allegiance to the legitimate authority with a full understanding that the rule Jesus brought was incompatible with the operating principles of earthly systems.

But what is this heavenly kingdom? My answer will begin in this chapter and continue in the next one. By way of preview, I want to summarize a few of its features that contrast this kingdom with the way human societies have functioned:

1. *Status*: Worldly systems that elevate some people to superior status and relegate others to lowly status are rejected. The struggle for status is replaced by a concern to do humble service for the good of the community.

2. *Power*: Instead of societal power structures that work to the advantage of those in elevated positions, but oppress others, the kingdom of God prioritizes justice and mercy for the weak and vulnerable.

3. *Violence*: In Jesus's kingdom animosity toward enemies and retaliation for wrongs gives way to forgiveness and compassion. The way of love replaces the way of violence.

I will be focusing on the first two features of the kingdom in this chapter and the third in the next chapter. These prescriptions are not the only things

Jesus taught about God's kingdom, but they are central to his vision of God's reign.

Jesus is often understood as teaching new standards of individual behavior, standards that are harder to live up to than previous ones. But this way of describing things misses something vital. Jesus is proposing a kind of reorganization of social life to correspond to God's intentions for humanity. Individual change will be needed, but the individual behaviors he describes should not be seen in isolation from a community that is constituted by values that differ from those that have structured previous societies. In other words, more than individual change is involved.

But how is this new order to come about? In renouncing the way of violence, Jesus does not seek to bring about this change through coercive means dictated by someone at the top. Instead, he symbolically chooses twelve disciples who represent a new Israel. It seems likely that Jesus anticipated that Jewish leaders of the time would not accept his message, but that he expected his followers to form new communities that would embody the values of the kingdom. There are hints in Jesus's teaching about how these counter-cultural communities may affect the larger society. He compares the kingdom of God to yeast, something very small that nevertheless permeates a larger body (Matt 13:33). Or it will be like a mustard seed, something seemingly insignificant that has unexpected growth (Matt 13:31–32). From one point of view the signs of the new order may be barely discernible, but the end result will be significant.

New Testament writers will describe earthly powers as defeated by what Jesus has accomplished. But even if the seeds of their destruction have been planted, their final defeat must lie in the future. Nevertheless, followers of Jesus are invited to live in anticipation of what God will bring to fulfillment. In doing so, they get a taste of the kingdom of God as a present reality. When we love our enemies, practice forgiveness, lift up the broken-hearted, and show compassion to the weak and defenseless, we are sampling the kind of life God intends for humanity. As we open ourselves to this new way of living, we also become vehicles through which the world can recognize and be challenged by an alternative to business as usual.

INCLUDING THE WRONG PEOPLE

Matthew, Mark, and Luke all record a visit by Jesus to his hometown synagogue in Nazareth. In Luke's Gospel we are given an account of Jesus reading a scriptural text from Isa 61. Luke quotes the text as follows:

> The Spirit of the Lord is upon me,

> because he has anointed me
> > to bring good news to the poor.
> He has sent me to proclaim release to the captives
> > and recovery of sight to the blind,
> > to let the oppressed go free,
> to proclaim the year of the Lord's favor (Luke 4:18–19).

Luke then says that Jesus rolls the scroll up, sits down (as rabbis traditionally did when they taught), and announces, "Today this scripture has been fulfilled in your hearing" (Luke 4:21). At first, the reception seems warm, but then the congregation apparently begins to question his interpretations and to challenge him to validate his claims by performing miraculous acts. What they are questioning becomes clearer when Jesus cites two instances from Hebrew Scriptures in which prophets of God act compassionately toward gentiles: rendering aid to a widow and healing a commander of an enemy army. At this point, the people become enraged and try to throw him off a cliff (presumably to stone him).

Why do those who hear Jesus become enraged? Apparently, they had no problem with Jesus announcing that he is fulfilling a Messianic text (at least if he will prove himself). But he gives an account of the Messiah's mission that they cannot stomach. In the first place, he stops reading from Isaiah just before a passage that speaks of a day of vengeance. From their point of view, he leaves out a vital part of what will occur. The day of vengeance was widely understood by Jews of the time as divine retribution directed against gentiles. There would be blessings for Israel and punishment for other nations. Luke's description suggests that Jesus sees his mission differently. Perhaps his understanding is informed by a different part of the book of Isaiah that describes Israel as a "light to the nations" through whom God's blessing will be given to all people. But this audience doesn't want love and mercy to be extended to foreigners who they think deserve God's wrath.

It is not the only time that Jesus arouses opposition by including the wrong people. Much of his conflict with Jewish religious leaders seems to center around their indignation that he was not drawing the lines properly between those who should receive God's blessings and those who should not. Instead of commending those who are zealous about observing God's law, he has table fellowship with tax collectors who are in league with foreign occupiers. He welcomes common people who have not studied the law of God and are not diligent about observing its requirements, and he even befriends women with questionable sexual morality. Jesus acts as if those who are unworthy of God's blessings are as important as those with great religious and social status.

In response to complaints about overly inclusive policies, Jesus tells the parable of the prodigal son (Luke 15:11–32). The father in the story (representing God) is gracious toward a son who has shown extreme disrespect toward the father and brought shame on the family. According to one interpreter familiar with Middle Eastern culture, this son's asking for his inheritance from the father is the equivalent of saying he wishes the father were dead.[2] When the son returns home, hat in hand, the father amazingly receives him joyfully, even throwing a lavish party. The elder brother who represents the religious leaders who think God should do as they do and take a hard line toward those who don't measure up, is outraged that the younger brother is forgiven and welcomed instead of punished. The elder brother thinks that he is the one who deserves a party, not his despicable brother.

Jesus's welcoming attitudes toward those who fall on the wrong side of status and respectability lines correspond to the kind of kingdom he has announced in which the doors have been thrown open to all. It is a kingdom in which the divisions that support a sense of superiority to others are knocked down. In one of the earliest of New Testament writings, Paul would declare about the Christian community, "There is no longer Jew or Greek, there is no longer slave or free, there is no longer male or female; for all of you are one in Christ Jesus" (Gal 3:28). It goes without saying that Christians have often been far from achieving the sort of unity portrayed here. But it seems clear that New Testament writers recognized that the Christian community was intended to be one in which the categories that divide us are less important than what we have in common.

It is hard to overestimate how much of the world's evil comes about through internalizing distinctions between our kind of people and others who are different. We live in a world still dominated by tribal attitudes where we think, "My people are not the problem. It's those others." Hostility sometime leads to war or other forms of violence, but even when it does not, people often think that cruel attitudes and actions toward outsiders are fully justified. The Jews of Jesus's time sometimes showed their contempt for gentiles by labeling them as pigs, and, of course, gentiles had corresponding insults. That kind of contempt for other groups is pervasive in human life, even when we disguise it with overt politeness. Jesus envisions a community in which distinctions between "us and them" that become the basis for looking down on others are overcome. Through being the kind of community in which those who are excluded are welcomed, the church bears witness to a kind of order that contrasts with standard practice.

---

2. Bailey, *Jesus Through Middle Eastern Eyes*, 281.

The problem is not just with outsiders. Even within a community there can be hierarchies that establish some people as superior to others. When Paul says that in Christ there is no longer Jew and Greek, male and female, slave and free, he shows a grasp of the way the new order initiated by Jesus is beginning to break down some of the distinctions that relegate some members of a community to an inferior status. However, it will take time before the implications of challenging social hierarchies sinks in. For example, women no doubt gained a freedom within the Christian community that was unprecedented. But the effects of a male-dominated culture were not simply erased. Only as people begin to realize the corrosive effects of social roles that give some people a subordinate status will they see the need to reject the reigning paradigms. Similarly, erasing the distinction between slave and free won't be just a matter of having civil relations between slaves and masters in the same congregation. It calls for realizing that this kind of power over other people conflicts with the Christian message and needs to be repudiated. It will take a long time for the import of the gospel message to sink in, but the yeast of the kingdom will eventually produce changes in how people think about such matters.

LIBERATING THE OPPRESSED

You cannot genuinely welcome those who have been excluded without dealing with the conditions that keep them from full participation in the community. In the visit to the Nazareth synagogue, Luke describes Jesus as reading from a text in Isaiah about liberation. In its original context the main passage from Isa 61 deals with release of the Jewish exiles from Babylon, though the prophet is also describing what will happen in the Messianic age. The image of release from exile was a widely accepted metaphor in Jesus's time for the kind of liberation the Messiah would bring. The quotation in Luke combines words from Isa 61 with words from Isa 42:7 about opening the eyes of the blind and from Isa 58:6 about setting the oppressed free. The various groups who will be liberated could be thought of as distinct. However, there is merit in thinking of all the people described in this text as falling under the category "the poor." The blind, as well as others Jesus healed, were often relegated to the position of beggars, and the captives mentioned in Luke are likely those who had been forced into servitude because of debt.

The reference to proclaiming "the year of the Lord's favor" in this text is widely recognized as a reference to the year of Jubilee. The Jubilee year described in Leviticus was prescribed to occur every fiftieth year when all land would revert to its original owner and debt slaves would be released.

We have no strong evidence that Jubilee was ever practiced in Israel, but even if it was not, it expressed a kind of ideal written into sacred documents that wealth and power should not be allowed to accumulate to the point where some people are forced into poverty and servitude without any remedy. The Jubilee prescription reflects the view that there are limits to the kind of economic inequality that could be tolerated. At a certain point, there should be a kind of reset.[3]

It has been proposed that Jesus was announcing just such a reset and that reinstating the practice of Jubilee was the good news he brought to those who were trapped in a system that kept them in perpetual poverty and put them at risk of slavery.[4] However, the reference to Jubilee in this text may be more of an image of liberation than a literal proposal. Even so, there is good reason to think that Jesus deplored the kind of system that resulted in the inequalities that Jubilee was supposed to remedy. Jesus preached in the tradition of the prophets who spoke scathingly about the rich taking advantage of the poor. He openly condemned the religious elite for practicing piety while acting greedily to "devour widows' houses" (Luke 20:47). His climactic symbolic act of overturning the tables of the moneychangers in the temple where he speaks of a "den of robbers" reveals his anger at a religious system that tolerated systematic exploitation of the poor.

In addition to condemning uses of power that treated the poor unjustly, Hebrew Scriptures also implore Israelites to show mercy to fellow members of the community. The book of Deuteronomy instructs Israelites to lend to their needy neighbor even when they know that the debts will be cancelled by a year of Jubilee (Deut 15:9). It is enough that a member of the community is in need:

> If there is anyone in need, a member of your community in any one of the towns within the land that the Lord your God is giving you, do not be hard-hearted or tight-fisted toward your needy neighbor. You should rather open your hand, willingly lending enough to meet the need, whatever it may be (Deut 15:7–8).

---

3. Kraybill explains the problem in Jesus's time as follows: "Much of Galilee was divided into large estates owned by wealthy merchants and Sadducees living in Jerusalem and by Gentile landowners who lived outside of Palestine. The parables of Jesus attest to this condition with their numerous references to absentee landowners who placed a steward in charge of their property . . . Peasant farmers also owned small plots of land. But they were gradually losing ownership of their plots because of debts . . . Often the peasant family would end up trapped on the plot, working as day laborers for the wealthy and absentee landholders." Kraybill, *Upside-Down Kingdom*, 86.

4. Yoder cites André Trocmé's proposal of the idea as worthy of consideration in *Politics of Jesus*, 36–37.

So, when Jesus speaks of good news to the poor, we can say that at very least he was speaking of a restoration of the kind of just treatment and mercy prescribed in Hebrew Scripture. One of his parables describes a rich man who feasted sumptuously every day, but was indifferent to a poor and diseased beggar at the gate of his house (Luke 16:19–31). His callousness is antithetical to the concern for neighbor expected in kingdom communities.

N. T. Wright claims that while Jesus was not expecting the nation as a whole to reinstitute the practice of Jubilee,

> *he expected his followers to live by the Jubilee principle among themselves.* He expected and taught that they should forgive one another not only 'sins' but also debts. This may help to explain the remarkable practice in the early church whereby resources were pooled ... Acts 4:34 echoes the description of the sabbatical year described in Deuteronomy 15:4.[5]

The "good news for the poor," found in Luke's Gospel is surely not just that God will forgive their sins, so they can go to heaven. It points toward a community in which those who have been oppressed receive what they need. Furthermore, Jesus's parable of the Good Samaritan makes it clear that the understanding of the neighbor to be helped extends widely.

CHRISTIANS AND THE EXCLUDED

It is painful to recognize that people who think of themselves as Christians have often failed to be the kind of community Jesus envisioned. Rather than being protectors of those whom society has marginalized, they have often supported systems that preserve their own privilege, but result in perpetual cycles of misery for those who have little. It is not that they don't believe in aiding people in need. It is rather that their sense of what should be done is filtered through ideologies they have been socialized to accept. In American society people who are well off tend to think that they deserve their position and are often blind to obstacles faced by those who are less favored. If they think about discrimination, for example, it is in terms of intentional acts rather than the unconscious biases perpetuated by social conditioning or structural inequalities built into the functioning of the criminal justice system, education, hiring and promotion practices, housing options, and healthcare.

There are biblical passages that associate prosperity with God's blessing and suffering with God's punishment. When Jesus expressed doubt

---

5. Wright, *Jesus and the Victory*, 295.

about whether a rich person could even enter the kingdom of God, he was challenging this simplistic ideology. When he devoted much of his ministry to healing those who were afflicted, he was rejecting the view that their suffering was God's will. When he told parables that were critical of the rich, he was putting the well-off on notice that they couldn't be complacent about the plight of the poor. When he spoke of the first being last and the last first, he was saying that the changes needed would overturn ingrained expectations about how things should be.

Christians need to learn new biases. When they hear ideas used to justify and perpetuate wealth and privilege for the few, they need to learn to look at these claims from the point of view of those who have little opportunity to participate in the goods of society. When they hear stories of people who are struggling, they need to imagine what it would be like to be in a position where there are few good options. When they hear the laments of employers who claim that they can't find anyone willing to work, they need to question whether they are getting the full story. When they find themselves thinking in stereotypical ways about people of lower classes, they need to remind themselves that they are thinking about people who are precious to God.

When Jesus delivered good news about the kingdom of God, he realized it wasn't news that everyone would think good. For those who were satisfied with a social structure that provided them with elite status, it was more of a threat. Perhaps we shouldn't be surprised that it was the well-placed in society who orchestrated his death. If we think of the Christian message as concerned with the next life, but leaving life here and now to continue unchanged, we may not understand why Jesus provoked such animosity. But it is clear for anyone with eyes to see that Jesus was taking the side of the poor and making things uncomfortable for those with wealth and power. If people with wealth and power are not uncomfortable with Jesus's message today, we might suspect that they haven't heard it well.

Jesus taught that we should pray for God's will to be done on earth. We may have trouble recognizing God's will when we mix it with messages our own society gives us. We may worry about being out of sync with others in our social class when we question what is often taken for granted. But being a part of a Christian community is not about preserving our own comfort and security. It is about acting according to the counter-cultural values that represent God's order for human life. If giving testimony to God's kingdom by what we say and what we do creates animosity from those who are comfortable with the status quo, we should recall that this was the same kind of response Jesus received and the kind he predicted for those who were willing to follow him.

CHAPTER 15

God's New Order
Enemies and Violence

ONE OF THE UNIVERSITY courses I taught regularly was called "Ethics and Good Living." In this course we studied various thinkers who developed accounts of how to live a good life. In addition to readings from both historical and contemporary philosophers, the anthology I used for the course had a section in which various biblical texts were used to represent the teachings of Jesus. These texts included selections from the "Sermon on the Mount" and the parable of the "Good Samaritan." My classes at a state university included people who had no background in the Bible, as well as students who brought with them an understanding that was based on what they had heard in church.

When we looked at texts from the Gospels where Jesus teaches some things that seem pretty demanding such as turning the other cheek and loving your enemies, there was considerable discussion about what the teachings meant. Some thought that they called for overriding very strong natural inclinations and that acting according to these teachings would be extraordinarily difficult. Others thought they could limit the application of what was called for so that it wasn't quite as demanding as it might initially seem. However, most agreed Jesus was teaching a way of living that was strikingly different from how people usually act and that most people, including most Christians, do not really attempt to live according to his instructions.

I asked whether it is important for someone who claims to be a Christian to try to follow Jesus's teachings. Some said yes, but a significant number of Christian students thought that obeying the most difficult instructions was not really expected. They said that Jesus didn't actually intend for people to do what he taught, but rather to realize how far short they fell of God's standards, so that they would repent and be saved by God's grace. In other words, they thought that the teachings were intended to reveal human sinfulness, rather than to serve as instruction about in how to live.

I typically suggested to the class that there was something a little odd about claiming to be a follower of Jesus, but not trying to live in the way he taught. By this time in the course, we had read numerous ethical teachers. Some of them advocated ways of living that were very demanding, requiring disciplined retraining of habitual ways of thinking and acting, which could not be accomplished without sustained commitment. No one had suggested when we read these other thinkers that they were not really trying to get people to live as they taught. So, I asked how plausible it was that Jesus did not really intend his followers to behave as he instructed them. After all, didn't he say that living by his teachings was like building a house on a sturdy foundation? (Matt 7:24–27)

The tendency to minimize the importance of Jesus as a teacher is a byproduct of how the Christian message is often presented. Dallas Willard characterizes the messages that dominate conservative Christianity as "gospels of sin management."[1] They represent being forgiven as the all-important concern and understand forgiveness as a transaction that is independent of any behavioral change. To people who have heard this kind of message, talking about obeying Jesus's teaching can sound as if you are adding an extra requirement to something that is a gift of God. But that reaction is the result of an excessively narrow understanding of God's purposes. If we think that God's concern is not just to grant an entrance pass to heaven, but to offer abundant life now, it should not be surprising that experiencing this kind of life might depend on following some instructions.

Brian Zahnd says that many who accept Christ have "crafted a religion" that separates the Jesus who died on the cross from the "radical ideas" he taught that got him crucified.[2] Jesus is accepted as savior, but it is imagined that his teaching is somehow extraneous to his main mission of dying on the cross. This way of thinking gets things backward. Jesus's death on the cross was a consequence of his faithfulness to his main mission of proclaiming the kingdom of God. He said that the kingdom had come as a present reality and invited his followers to experience the kingdom by participating in a community that embraces the alternative way of living his teaching

---

1. Willard, *Divine Conspiracy*, 35–59.
2. Zahnd, *Farewell to Mars*, 33.

describes. His willingness to give up his own life is an expression of his own commitment to act toward his enemies in the way he had taught kingdom communities to act. When we accept salvation through the cross, we join Jesus in accepting the way of life that led to the cross. In this chapter I will be focusing on what Jesus says about dealing with enemies.

THOSE WHO TREAT YOU BADLY

When other people treat us badly, the typical reaction is anger. Sometimes our anger leads to fantasies about how those who have caused us to suffer should be punished. A significant number of Psalms contain such fantasies, usually in the form of prayers for God to bring misery on those who have done the Psalmist wrong. Here is an example:

> Let their table be a trap for them,
> a snare for their allies.
> Let their eyes be darkened so that they cannot see,
> and make their loins tremble continually. . . .
> Pour out your indignation on them,
> and let your burning anger overtake them.
> May their camp be a desolation;
> let no one live in their tents. . . .
> Let them be blotted out of the book of the living . . .
> (Ps 69:22-25, 28)

Most of us would probably be embarrassed to pray such a prayer. When Scripture passages are read in church, we tend to omit those that call for harsh vengeance against our enemies. But we understand the sentiment. When people have hurt us or hurt those we love, it is easy to find ourselves wishing that they suffer for it. The kind of policy that most people in our culture regard as normal is doing good to those who treat us well, but retaliating against those who have harmed us.

But what kind of retaliation would be sufficient? Sometimes we think that those who have treated us badly deserve the worst kind of punishment. The Psalmist quoted above thinks that these oppressors should be made to suffer greatly and then killed. The appeal is for God to bring this judgment. But if God doesn't bring punishment in a timely manner, we are often ready to take on the job ourselves to make those who have harmed us pay the consequences of their misdeeds. Usually this means acting in anger, but sometimes it is more cold-blooded. One of my former students announced to a class that he lived by the advice, "Don't get mad; get even."

In Hebrew Scriptures there is a rule that is presumably designed to keep retaliation from getting out of hand. It is the rule that what is done in retaliation is not to exceed the severity of the injury. So, according to this rule, having your own eye gouged out might justify gouging out the perpetrator's eye in return. More generally, "life for life, eye for eye, tooth for tooth, hand for hand, foot for foot, burn for burn, wound for wound, stripe for stripe" (Exod 21:24–25). Application of the rule might seem brutal, but think of such retaliatory justice as a way of limiting the kind of harm that might be inflicted in response to what others do. Of course, it is not always possible to rectify wrongs in the way this rule suggests. What is the appropriate punishment for someone who has raped you or destroyed your reputation by spreading false stories or violated your trust? Furthermore, retaliating can involve more than individual action. What if the one who caused the injury has the protection of some group of people? Is it then justified to gather your friends and attack that group to gain vengeance? That reaction might lead to many people being harmed, and the injuries inflicted in the pursuit of justice could become part of a continuing cycle of violence.

Jesus offers a way out of this kind of cycle, but his way will strike some people as foolish or even shameful. He proposes dropping the need to retaliate against those who wrong you. In response to the old rule of "eye for eye, tooth for tooth," Jesus says not to resist an evil doer (Matt 5:39). At least, that is the usual translation of the text. But the word translated as "resist" is used most often in the Greek translation of Hebrew Scriptures as a technical term for warfare. Some translators say the Matthew text should be rendered as "do not violently resist." The instruction likely deals with the kind of resistance where you respond to an attack or an affront by taking a stance equivalent to that of the aggressor, meeting force with force. But what is Jesus's alternative? Part of the answer is found in three examples he offers of refusing to play the oppressor's game.[3]

The first example is well known: "But if anyone strikes you on the right cheek, turn the other also" (Matt 5:39). (This saying is also in Luke, but without the mention of which cheek.) Commentators say that the reference to a strike on the right cheek refers to a backhanded blow that is intended as an insult. There is reason to think that the example refers to a strike by a social superior against someone with inferior status. Recall that Jesus's audience would have consisted mostly of those who were low on the social ladder and would be familiar with the kind of treatment intended to put them in their place. So, what is the proposed response? We could say that it

---

3. My discussion of these examples is indebted to Walter Wink. See his *Engaging the Powers*, 175–93.

involves giving someone who has struck you the opportunity to strike again. But think of the situation from the viewpoint of people familiar with being treated with contempt by those with greater power. What are their options? They could try to fight back, likely a futile and self-defeating response. They could passively accept the blow with bowed heads. What Jesus seems to offer is an alternative that is neither forceful retaliation nor servility. In turning the other cheek, the victim is symbolically refusing to be just a victim, but taking the initiative in an unexpected way. The next blow might come, but if it does, it will now be an attack on someone who refrains from striking back, but has removed the option of another backhanded blow delivered to an inferior.

The second example involves someone who uses the force of law to take something from a poor person: " . . . if anyone wants to sue you and take your coat, give your cloak as well" (Matt 5:40). The background for understanding this text is in Deut 24. There we are told that that one who has made a loan can take the debtor's outer garment as a pledge that the loan will be repaid, but has to return it each night, if the one who owes the loan needs it as a covering for sleep. So, in this case we are imagining a creditor who is using the power of the court to extract almost everything from a poor person. Going to ridiculous extremes, the creditor wants the tunic or inner garment. What does Jesus suggest? He says to let the one demanding the tunic have everything by relinquishing not only the tunic, but the only other item of clothing, the outer garment. In this case the symbolic act of stripping naked looks like a way of exposing the one making these outrageous demands to public shame. Again, we have a response to abusive power by taking the initiative in an unexpected, but nonviolent way, rather than just submitting passively to this kind of treatment.

The third example also involves dealing with someone with power over you. In this case it is a Roman soldier who is entitled to conscript a local peasant to carry his pack. Doing so was particularly offensive to a people who hated the presence of these foreign occupiers of their nation. The Roman military code allowed this kind of enforced labor, but limited what could be required to carrying the pack for a mile. So, what does Jesus suggest? " . . . if anyone forces you to go one mile, go also the second mile" (Matt 5:41). At one level, the teaching is to submit to power. But there is something subversive about submitting in a way that actually puts the soldier in violation of the regulation that limited his power of conscription. What we seem to have is a victim of oppressive power who takes control of the situation.

These three examples are apparently offered as alternatives to forcefully resisting those who use power in an oppressive way. Walter Wink argues that Jesus's examples show us an alternative to both violence and passivity that he calls a "third way." The third way involves resisting objectionable uses of power, but without adopting the coercive methods of the powerful. Instead of meeting force with force, we are to act in a way that is "assertive and yet nonviolent."[4]

But perhaps it is a leap to say that these examples amount to a general teaching of nonviolence. It might be if we were reading this text in isolation. However, there are three considerations that make the idea that Jesus was teaching nonviolent resistance compelling. First, Jesus was speaking in a context where violence against Roman oppression was always near the surface. He clearly opposed this way of dealing with the problem. In fact, he predicted that the Jewish proclivity toward violent resistance would lead to the destruction of Jerusalem, a prediction that was fulfilled within forty years. Second, what Jesus taught about forgiveness and about loving enemies fits best with understanding him to be rejecting violent responses. Third, we should read these examples in the light of Jesus's own refusal to respond with violence when he faced the coercive use of power that led to his crucifixion. Jesus understood as part of his vocation the need to accept this treatment, rather than meeting force with force, and he told his followers that they needed to be willing to take up the cross themselves.

LOVE FOR ENEMIES

Matthew reports Jesus as saying, "Love your enemies and pray for those who persecute you" (Matt 5:44). Luke records the saying as, "Love your enemies, do good to those who hate you, bless those who curse you, pray for those who abuse you" (Luke 6:27–28). Luke puts this teaching next to other sayings that taken together suggest a willingness to lay down concern for protecting your own interests that is likely to strike most people as carried to absurd lengths. Immediately after this saying, Luke cites teachings about turning the other cheek when someone strikes you, giving away your shirt to someone who takes your coat, giving to anyone who begs, and not seeking the return of what someone else takes from you. He sums it all up with the saying, "Do unto others as you would have them do unto you" (Luke 6:31). The enemy is apparently no exception to a general pattern of responding to each person with an openhearted kindness without consideration of personal benefit.

From the examples of nonretaliation in Matthew, we can conclude that Jesus teaches dealing with abusive uses of power by acting in surprising

---

4. Wink, *Powers That Be*, 101.

ways. But the examples alone don't tell us what attitude to take toward the oppressor. Conceivably, you might hate and silently curse the other person while turning the other cheek. But in the saying about loving enemies, it appears that Jesus is rejecting not only the use of force, but also hostile attitudes toward the enemy. The friendly attitudes that we aspire to when dealing with those we think of as neighbors are to be extended to enemies as well.

I doubt that what is taught here is that we are to have warm-hearted feelings toward everyone. However, including the enemy in the class of neighbor may mean that we refuse to write off the enemy as just wicked. But what is the alternative, particularly when we recognize that people do very wicked things? Perhaps it is a bias toward remembering our own failings and thinking of even the worst people as redeemable. Such an attitude might be contrasted with the common tendency to demonize those who oppose us. When nations go to war, part of the preparation for bringing violence on the enemy is a process of dehumanization. We learn to think of the enemy as subhuman, outside the limits of decent society. So, maybe we could think of loving the enemy as a call to deliberately humanize the enemy. Rather than magnifying the sense of otherness, we strive to think of the enemy as one of us.

In an amplification of the command to love the enemy found in both Matthew and Luke, we are told to pray for those who are treating us badly. We are to ask God to bless them, which is often the last thing we want to happen. Notice that the instruction is the opposite of the cursing of the enemy we find in some of the Psalms. If these prayers are not to be utterly hypocritical, they have to mean getting to the point where hostility towards the enemy gives way to a concern for the enemy's good. Such a shift need not mean endorsing the enemy's behavior, but it does involve laying down the need for retribution. In other words, it means a readiness to forgive.

In both Matthew and Luke this kind of response to enemies is described as an imitation of what God does. God, we are told in Matthew, sends sun and rain on good and bad people alike (Matt 5:45). Luke says that God is kind to the ungrateful and the wicked (Luke 6:45). In other words, there is a kind of indiscriminateness about God's benefits that is not based on what we deserve. We may, like the Psalmist, long for offenders to get God's judgment, but the God revealed in Jesus's teaching seems to be less concerned with retributive justice that punishes the offender than with a kind of restorative justice that brings those who have strayed back into the fold. Jesus apparently believed that mercy and forgiveness, in contrast to Pharisaic condemnation, are the way to try to draw an offender back.

The instruction to respond to enemies without malice is not just in the Gospels. Paul echoes the teaching in Matthew and Luke when he says, "Do not repay anyone evil for evil" and " . . . never avenge yourselves" (Rom 12:17, 19). Paul says that we can leave vengeance to God. He instructs Christians, " . . . if your enemies are hungry, feed them, if they are thirsty, give them something to drink" (Rom 12:20). Paul does suggest that this kind of behavior may have an effect on the enemy's conscience. But whether it does or not, he teaches, "Do not be overcome by evil, but overcome evil with good" (Rom 12:21). So, the counter-cultural New Testament teaching is not to play the enemy's game of tit for tat, but instead to respond to the enemy's abuse with acts of kindness.

This way of responding to enemies can seem barely conceivable. But it is a core part of the identity of some Christian communities. In 2006 Charles Roberts took his arsenal of guns into an Amish schoolhouse in rural Pennsylvania. He sent the teacher and boys away, but kept ten girls between the ages of six and thirteen in the building. He then proceeded to shoot each of the girls in the head before turning a gun on himself. Five of the girls died, and five were left in critical condition.

Roberts left behind a stunned wife Amy, along with their three children. Within hours of the incident, members of the Amish community arrived at the Roberts house, bringing with them gifts of food and offering their forgiveness for the horrendous act of violence. They promised continued support for the family and later for the parents of Charles Roberts. A few days later at the burial of the one who had brought such grief to their community, nearly forty Amish people were present, offering comfort to members of the Roberts family. The Amish showed no hint of hostility and no interest in retaliation. As a community, they were shaped by a tradition of nonviolence, and they had internalized the teaching to respond to evil with goodness. It was not a matter for discussion among them. They considered no other option.[5]

This schoolhouse shooting was one among what have become all too numerous acts of senseless violence. The tragedy of the event was not erased by what happened in the aftermath. The parents and the whole community still had to live with the loss of their precious little girls. But the slaughter of the children wasn't the whole story. What stands out is a response to evil that is strikingly different from the standard responses of anger and retaliation. What stands out is a community who lived in accordance with the teachings of one who told them to love their enemies. The tragedy is

---

5. Kraybill, *Amish Grace*.

undeniable, but so also are glimmers of a way of life that exhibits God's intentions for human beings.

CHRISTIANS AND NONVIOLENCE

In the first three centuries of the Christian era, we find a consistent repudiation of violence by Christians. Some Christian writers speak against all killing of other people. No Christian writer during this period approves of participating in military service or serving as a government official who might have to invoke the death penalty. Second-century apologist Justin Martyr says of Christians, "We who once killed each other not only do not make war on each other, but in order not to lie or deceive our inquisitors we gladly die for the confession of Christ."[6] The anti-Christian satirist Celsus criticized Christians in the second century for their disloyalty in refusing to serve in the military, raising the alarm about what would happen if their attitude was more widespread. Tertullian near the end of the second century wrote, "We are equally forbidden to wish ill, to do ill, to speak ill, and to think ill of all men . . . If injured, we are forbidden to retaliate lest we become as bad ourselves . . . "[7] Tertullian's advice to a soldier who accepts Christianity is to quit the army or accept martyrdom. Until the time of Constantine Jesus's teaching was widely understood to mean that being a follower of Christ meant renouncing the use of violence.

A shift occurs when Christianity was accepted as the official religion of the Roman Empire. Theologians after this time offered a qualified acceptance of war. The most significant of these theologians was Augustine who, building on Cicero's thought, developed the "just war" tradition that specified conditions under which war could be permitted, as well as rules that limited what combatants could legitimately do. It is striking that Augustine himself understood the teachings of Jesus to forbid even killing in self-defense, but he thought that there could be some justification of resorting to violence in defense of the innocent. Though there have been pacifist groups in Christian tradition after the fourth century, the dominant view in the church since Augustine has been that armed violence can be justified under some circumstances and that Christians may participate in just wars.

This shift in Christian thinking corresponds to changing conditions in which Christians were integrated into society in such a way that they had the opportunity to occupy positions of power. In this new kind of situation, they came to think that their task was to use power responsibly and to be

---

6. Justin, *Apology*, 266.
7. Tertullian, *Apology*, 45.

realistic about responding to violence. The criteria for just war are intended as a reasoned way to mitigate violence. In retrospect these criteria have not been effective in achieving this end. For the most part, Christians have been willing to go along with whatever wars and means of waging war their nation supported. Christians living under democratic regimes have often had difficulty thinking that there could be a real conflict between the goals of their nation and the goals of the kingdom of God. They have rarely even been troubled by the tension between Jesus's teaching to love the enemy and their own support of bringing violent destruction on the enemy. Nor have they advocated strongly for restricting what could be done by combatants. The existence of just war criteria limiting the conduct of war did not prevent a huge majority of the American public from thinking that it was justified to carry out a nuclear attack against the civilian population of two Japanese cities.

In the early centuries Christians recognized that they were embracing a way of life that was at odds with the dominant culture. In the book of Revelation, Rome was portrayed symbolically as Babylon, the evil empire from Hebrew Scripture, and as the Beast. It was taken as obvious that this empire was built on principles opposed to God's rule. Like all earthly kingdoms, it was built on violence. The kingdom of God would ultimately prevail not by violent means, but through the subversive kind of power of a community built on forgiveness of the enemy and returning good for evil. The members of this community were committed to the view that it was better to suffer violence than to inflict it.

In striking contrast, contemporary Christians tend to understand their faith through the lens of their identity as patriotic citizens who are committed to some understanding of the national interest. Rather than recognizing that worldly kingdoms, including democratic nations, are built on uses of power that are antithetical to the gospel message, Christians have typically viewed their own national agendas as expressions of a righteous cause. Gregory Boyd points out what should be obvious:

> No version of the kingdom of the world, however comparatively good it may be, can protect its self-interests while loving its enemies, turning the other cheek, going the extra mile, or blessing those who persecute it. Yet loving our enemies and blessing those who persecute us is precisely what kingdom-of-God citizens are called to do. It's what it means to be a Christian.[8]

The choice is between a vision of the church as a counter-cultural community that seeks to fulfill its mission by living in a way that contrasts

---

8. Boyd, *Myth of a Christian Nation*, 54.

sharply with the values of society or a church that adjusts to society's values to gain power or influence that can be used for good. The Amish are an example of the former approach. Their concern is to be a faithful witness to the message of Jesus, even if it puts them at odds with the dominant culture.

Interpreters of the Christian message in the early centuries understood Jesus to teach the way of nonviolence. In the last fifty years or so a significant number of New Testament scholars have concluded that they were largely correct. Richard Hays writes, " . . . from Matthew to Revelation we find a consistent witness against violence and a calling to the community to follow the example of Jesus in *accepting suffering* rather than *inflicting* it."[9] It might seem that such a teaching is too distant from human nature as we find it to be realistic. John Howard Yoder responds, "God broke through the borders of man's definition of what is human and gave a new, formative definition in Jesus"[10]

There is room for disputing whether violence might be justified in some circumstances. But what seems to me beyond dispute is that the church has strayed far away from its source teachings in endorsing the violence that permeates human society. We have been seduced by what Walter Wink calls the "myth of redemptive violence," the view that order and security comes only through the use of force to vanquish the evildoer. This idea is constantly reinforced by stories we use for entertainment in which the "good guys" violently defeat the "bad guys." As a result of absorbing an understanding that our culture accepts as obvious, we find it difficult to take seriously a message that tells us to resist evil through nonviolent means.

Responding to that message is not a purely intellectual matter. Embracing the way of nonviolence means a willingness to suffer at the hands of violent people. We may hope that God's love will prevail in the end, but in the meantime imitating Christ in laying down the instruments of violence may sometimes mean suffering and death. In the New Testament those who are faithful to the path of Jesus are told to expect suffering. It might seem like a hollow comfort to say as Paul did that the Christian life means fellowship in the suffering of Christ (Phil 3:10–11), but to think in this way means recognizing that we are engaged in a common mission, which means accepting the risk that goes with it. Peacemakers know that the human cycle of violence cannot be overcome by force. It can only be overcome through the witness of those who refuse to get caught up in the cycle of violence and demonstrate a better way.

---

9. Hays, *Moral Vision*, 332.
10. Yoder, *Politics of Jesus*, 101.

The new order Jesus described goes against much of what we have been socialized to accept. It overturns our assessments of status by making self-giving service the norm of true greatness. It upends our inclination to cultivate the rich and powerful by telling us to focus our attention on the poor and oppressed. It tells us to drop our concern with avenging ourselves and replace it with love for our enemies. If we think from the perspective of preserving our own privilege and power, accepting the way of Jesus looks threatening. But Jesus taught that it is only by giving up our hold on what seems to be important that we learn what is really important. Once we have taken to heart what it means to live as God intended, we may not be willing to settle for anything less.

CHAPTER 16

The Resurrection

I HAVE POINTED OUT in earlier chapters that interpreting biblical revelation can call for rejecting some things a biblical writer says. For example, you can accept biblical teaching about creation while rejecting the ancient scientific views in terms of which that teaching is expressed. You can recognize that biblical authors sometimes assume primitive views of God or questionable cultural views that can be rejected in the light of fuller revelation. However, you should not think that you can simply adjust biblical texts whenever they say things that do not fit with ideas you find appealing. Doing so sometimes results in losing what is central to biblical teaching.

People who adjust biblical teachings to conform to views that are widely accepted in their own time are often well intentioned. They may, for example, want to express the message in a way that makes it more plausible to their contemporaries by removing unnecessary barriers to accepting it. For instance, some have thought that miracle stories are the product of an outdated way of thinking that we can eliminate because it conflicts with our sense of things happening in accordance with scientific regularities. Doing so, it is suggested, helps us get to the heart of the message without getting hung up on problematic features that can be trimmed away. In the early 1800s Thomas Jefferson, influenced by the deism of his age, literally used a penknife and paste to make his own version of Scripture. He retained texts he found edifying, but removed stories about miraculous events, including the resurrection. You don't have to accept every miracle story in the Bible to take biblical revelation seriously. But approaching these texts with the assumption that scientifically inexplicable events don't occur threatens the coherency of a story that centers on God's action in the world. And there is one miracle story that seems absolutely essential. Without the resurrection of Jesus, the New Testament message becomes unintelligible.

THE NEW TESTAMENT UNDERSTANDING OF THE RESURRECTION

New Testament claims about resurrection are not just a generalized way of talking about life after death. In the ancient world people accepted various versions of life after death. Some thought of it as like the kind of shadowy existence that Homer ascribes to souls in Hades. Others, influenced by the thought of Plato, imagined liberation of the soul from the body, resulting in freedom from physical restraints so that we can achieve our true destiny. Talk about resurrection, however, involved a different vision of life after death. It meant some kind of reconstituted bodily existence. To many people outside of Judaism, such an idea seemed not only unlikely, but not particularly desirable. When Paul brings up the topic of resurrection in Athens, he immediately loses some of his audience (Acts 17:32).

In Judaism the hope of resurrection emerged fairly late. There is little mention in Hebrew Scriptures of any kind of life after death other than a sort of ghostly existence in *Sheol*, which was not something to look forward to. The focus of these writings is clearly on life in this world. However, in the centuries preceding the birth of Jesus, significant Jewish reflection about life after death arises. An important impetus for this thought was the question of the fate of faithful Jews who had died as martyrs. A view that came to be widely accepted was that there would be a general resurrection in the end times in which the whole person would be reconstituted in bodily form. Martha's comment to Jesus about Lazarus rising again in the resurrection on the last day (John 11:24) likely expresses this kind of belief.

It is in the context of this Jewish way of thinking about life after death that claims of followers of Jesus about his resurrection should be understood. When they said that God had raised Jesus from the dead, they were not saying that his soul had continued to exist after his death. They were saying that what was expected to occur in the last days for many people had happened to one particular individual. The authorities had killed Jesus, but God had brought him back to life in bodily form. Later in this chapter, I will consider their basis for making such a claim. But first I want to discuss the significance they attached to the resurrection of Jesus.

What did it mean to the followers of Jesus to think that God had raised him from the dead? First, it meant that *he was God's Messiah* (in Greek, Christ). Jesus had gathered disciples, and prior to the crucifixion at least some of them had believed that Jesus was the Messiah. But the crucifixion understandably erased all of that. What had happened in the crucifixion was what generally happened to failed messianic movements. The leader had been forcefully eliminated. If someone had claimed to believe that Jesus, though crucified by the Romans, was still the Messiah, the claim would have seemed nonsensical. The proof that he was not the Messiah was the fact that he had been executed by the ruling powers. But contrary to expectations, something happened that convinced these disciples that God had raised Jesus from the dead. In their eyes, it was as if God was declaring that despite all appearances, Jesus was the Messiah after all. The resurrection was like a divine stamp of approval on what Jesus had been doing and saying.

But the resurrection meant more than a vindication of Jesus. In his coming to life again, the followers of Jesus saw the *dawn of a new age*, which they connected with the prophetic hope in Hebrew Scripture for a new kind of world. What was supposed to happen only at the end of time had begun to happen now. Paul speaks of a *new creation* that God has begun through the Messiah. He declares the resurrection of Jesus to be the first fruits of what is to come (1 Cor 15:20). In Hebrew tradition the first fruits of the harvest were given in anticipation of the fuller harvest. The fuller harvest Paul expected includes raising others from the dead, but the fate of individuals was only part of it. He claimed that what happened in the resurrection was a precursor to a reconstruction of the created order. Furthermore, he regarded the resurrected Messiah as the key to understanding what God would do.

The New Testament uses different images to speak about what God intends to bring about. But the basic idea seems to go something like this: God had always intended for human beings to rule over creation. However, doing so wisely calls for being in harmony with God's purposes. The harmony we might have possessed has been disrupted by the human propensity for greed and violence. But in the coming of Jesus we see a human being who at last is fully receptive to the Spirit of God. God's plan is to remake human beings on the model of Jesus so that they can fulfill their role as bearers of the divine image. The ultimate remaking will be in a resurrected body like his, but in the meantime those who follow Jesus can voluntarily partake of his Spirit and live in the light of what is to come.

God's purposes, as Paul describes them, extend beyond human beings to a renewal of the whole created order: "For the creation waits with eager longing for the revealing of the children of God . . . in hope that the creation itself will be set free from its bondage to decay and will obtain the freedom of the glory of the children of God" (Rom 8:19–21). We do not get details about how this transformation of creation is to occur, but it seems to involve both human beings living in a way that is responsive to God's intentions for them, along with a renewed material order that somehow becomes free of decay and death.

Physicist and theologian John Polkinghorne describes the biblical expectation as follows: "The new creation represents the transformation of the universe when it enters freely into a new and closer relationship with its Creator, so that it becomes . . . suffused with the divine presence."[1] It might be asked why this better universe couldn't have been made initially. Polkinghorne's answer is that God's two acts of creation are not the same thing.[2] The "old creation" is God's bringing into being something finite that can exist "on its own." God sets up the evolutionary possibilities for a universe to "make itself." Suffering in that universe is the price of its independence. But, says Polkinghorne, a universe with this kind of independence may be "freely returned" to the Creator. How would such a universe be different? Perhaps we can only imagine. I imagine that an infusion of the divine presence might result in a new kind of relation between human beings and the natural order, resulting in an attunement with and control of nature that if we had it now would seem akin to magic. The physical world, including our bodies, would be responsive to our needs, and we would be attentive to and instrumental in bringing about the good of the ecological system. Given human life as it is now, such expanded control would undoubtedly be disastrous. But properly attuned to God's spirit, we could conceivably use our enhanced powers to become the co-creators God wants us to be.

The main point here is not to try to conceive what a new creation would be like, but to recognize that in the New Testament the resurrection of Jesus is not thought of as an isolated event, but as the first installment of what will be a different kind of order, an order in which created things become vessels through which God's Spirit can be expressed. In the meantime, until God's project is completed, we are told that there is work for the followers of Jesus to do. They are to be what Paul called the "body of Christ" on earth whose job is to continue the work Jesus had begun. The idea is not that human beings bring about the kingdom of God, but rather that they can participate in the work God is doing and will ultimately bring to completion. As N. T. Wright puts it, God's "renewal . . . of the creation . . . means that what we do in the present by way of justice and mercy and grace and forgiveness and healing and liberation . . . will not be lost but will be part of the eventual kingdom that God will make."[3]

---

1. Polkinghorne, *Faith of a Physicist*, 167.
2. Polkinghorne, *Faith of a Physicist*, 167.
3. In Stewart, *Resurrection of Jesus*, 42.

So, to the early followers of Jesus, the resurrection meant that Jesus was the Messiah and that the new creation had begun. It also meant that *Jesus has a unique authority*. In raising Jesus from the dead, they claimed, God had made him the *true Lord of this world*. Earthly rulers such as Caesar may claim authority, but the declaration that "Jesus is Lord" was understood by early Christians to mean that Jesus is the supreme authority. In what appears to be an early Christian hymn, the aftermath of Jesus's death on the cross is described as follows:

> Therefore God also highly exalted him
>   and gave him the name
> that is above every name,
>   so that at the name of Jesus
> every knee should bend,
>   in heaven and on earth and under the earth,
> and every tongue should confess
>   that Jesus Christ is Lord,
> to the glory of God the Father (Phil 2:9–11).

The claim that Jesus is the true Lord of this world is subversive. The rulers of this world claim authority and back up their claims with armed force. Christians believed that in raising Jesus from the dead, God has declared him to be the real king. It may seem ludicrous to claim that the real king is one without an army to enforce his will, but early Christians were convinced that despite the appearances, the crucifixion and the resurrection signaled the defeat of earthly powers. Until God's victory became clear to all, Christians were, according to their self-understanding, opposition cells who had given their allegiance to another ruler.[4]

The constellation of meanings that early Christians connected with the resurrection of Jesus was central to their identity. If you take away the resurrection, you undermine their understanding of who they are as a people. For these followers of Jesus, the resurrection message was the key to understanding what God is doing in the world. All of the sermons in the book of Acts are centrally proclamations of the resurrection. The apostle Paul was unequivocal about its indispensability. He says to the Corinthian church, "if Christ has not been raised, then our proclamation has been in vain and your faith has been in vain" (1 Cor 15:14). Removing the resurrection is like removing a part of a structure that results in the whole thing collapsing.

---

4. Wright, *Resurrection of the Son of God*, 728–31.

BUT CAN YOU BELIEVE THAT JESUS WAS RAISED?

The evidence relevant to deciding whether Jesus was raised from the dead comes primarily from the New Testament. Some people who accept the resurrection think that either everything New Testament writers say about what happened must be historically accurate or these accounts should be rejected altogether. Hence, they try to put all the details of the various resurrection accounts together into a single consistent story. Efforts of this sort tend to be strained and unconvincing. A more productive approach is to think of what New Testament writers say as testimony. Ordinarily we don't assume that testimony about what happened is useless unless it is completely accurate about everything. If you are on a jury, you can sometimes judge that a witness is credible about some aspects of what is reported, but mistaken or deceptive about other aspects. In reaching a verdict you weigh the overall testimony from multiple witnesses to determine whether it gives you enough reason to judge guilt or innocence. Similarly, biblical reports may enable us to make judgments about whether the resurrection occurred, even if there is uncertainty about the accuracy of some accounts or some details.

So, what does biblical testimony tell us about the resurrection? New Testament scholars say that the earliest written account of the resurrection of Jesus is in Paul's letters. In 1 Cor 15 Paul quotes what is usually taken to be a statement of Christian beliefs that had been put in fixed form and passed on to him within a few years of the crucifixion:

> For I handed on to you as of first importance what I in turn had received: that Christ died for our sins in accordance with the scriptures and that he was buried, and that he was raised on the third day in accordance with the scriptures and that he appeared to Cephas, then to the twelve. Then he appeared to more than five hundred brothers and sisters at one time, most of whom are still alive, though some have died. Then he appeared to James, then to all the apostles (1 Cor 15:3-7).

Paul adds to this statement a claim that the risen Jesus also appeared to him, presumably his Damascus Road experience. This early statement of the church's belief that Jesus was raised refers to multiple appearances to different individuals at different times, some of which were in groups, including one group that was fairly large. Paul also tells the Corinthian church that some of the original witnesses were still alive at the time of his writing.

It seems very likely that stories circulated in the Christian community describing particular resurrection appearances, but Paul does not include such stories in his letters. For accounts of what resurrection appearances were like, we have to turn to the Gospels. In addition to stories about appearances of Jesus, the Gospels also give us testimony about an empty tomb. The Gospel accounts were written later than Paul's letters, and there is some reason to suspect that they contain some legendary additions and features that may have been put in because they fit a particular Gospel writer's theological agenda. But there are also indications that they include elements of very early oral tradition. One striking indication is the role of women in the Gospel tradition. In the ancient world there was a tendency to discount what women reported as less reliable than the testimony of men. So, if you were inventing a story to confirm belief in the resurrection, you would not likely give women a featured role as witnesses. But the Gospel accounts portray women as the first witnesses of the empty tomb. The most plausible explanation of why women are included in these narratives is that there was a core oral tradition in the Christian community that reported the events in this fashion.

Another noticeable feature that emerges in multiple appearance stories in the Gospels is that there are differences between the resurrected Jesus and the pre-crucifixion Jesus. Again, if you were just inventing a story to convince people that Jesus had risen, would you complicate matters by describing him as different? Or would you include reports that some did not recognize him or that some doubted? Elements of this kind give us some reason to think that even if there is embellishment in these stories, what we have is shaped by a core tradition that is very early.[5] Scholars disagree about how much evidential value to give to accounts about the empty tomb, but a

---

5. The core tradition reporting that Jesus was changed coheres with Paul's theological analysis of what happened. Paul cites Jesus as the first instance of resurrection that prefigures a final resurrection of others. In describing what is involved, he calls the earthly body a "soulish body" (*soma psychikon*). This kind of body is what regulates our ordinary contact with the world. It is not just flesh, but flesh that has been given the breath of life. In contrast Paul uses the term *soma pneumaticon* to refer to the resurrection body. The usual translation is "spiritual body," but that translation is misleading if we are thinking of the term "spiritual" as a contrast to physical. The *soma pneumaticon* is after all a body. I follow scholars who think that the primary reference is to a body that is animated by the divine Spirit. We might speculate that Paul's thought on this new body arises from his own Damascus Road experience of the glorified Christ. If we read the Gospel stories through the lens of Paul's account, the portrayal of Jesus as having a body that is able to do things an ordinary human body cannot do fits with the idea that some kind of transformation has occurred. What we get both in Paul's account and in the Gospel accounts is the suggestion of both continuity between the earthly body and the resurrected body, as well as change.

significant number of biblical scholars judge that these accounts were part of the earliest testimony about the resurrection.[6]

While someone might doubt the truth of the resurrection accounts, it is harder to doubt that early Christians believed Jesus was raised from the dead. Why would a group of Jews change their day of worship from the Sabbath (Friday sundown to Saturday sundown) to Sunday apart from a conviction that God had done something of tremendous consequence on the first day of the week? Why would the followers of Jesus proclaim a message about the resurrection of Jesus that was bound to arouse opposition from Jewish authorities? Why would they persist in proclaiming this message even when it led to suffering and the risk of death? Why did they often accept death rather than backing down? Their behavior gives us strong reason to acknowledge that something happened that resulted in the early followers of Jesus confidently believing that he had been raised from the dead.

Of course, one explanation of how they came to such a firm belief is that they really did encounter the risen Jesus and that they had good reason to think that the tomb he had been buried in was empty. But it should go without saying that not everyone accepts this explanation. Many alternatives have been offered, including the claim that the followers of Jesus were engaged in a grand deception. However, if the resurrection is rejected, it seems more plausible to posit that the followers of Jesus sincerely thought that they had encountered the risen Jesus, but were mistaken. Different versions of this view can be recognized as elaborations of the idea that the appearances of Jesus were the product of factors that resulted in subjectively real experiences that were mistakenly taken to be objectively real.

Perhaps the most promising way to develop this kind of account is to claim that the appearances reported by the followers of Jesus were visionary experiences, rather than experiences produced by ordinary sensation caused by physical objects. One candidate for the kind of visionary experiences the disciples had is what have been called apparitions of the dead. There is evidence throughout human history and across cultures that people sometimes experience appearances of someone who has died. Surveys in fairly recent times have shown that the phenomenon is surprisingly common. Many of these experiences are described in ways that differ from the stereotypical idea of a ghostly appearance. The person who has died is seen as solid, heard to speak, and in rare cases touched.[7] Someone who doubts the resurrection could claim that resurrection appearances should

---

6. For a balanced critical discussion of arguments for and against the empty tomb see Allison, *Resurrecting Jesus*, 299–337.

7. Allison discusses apparitions of the dead in relation to the resurrection and cites a wide range of sources documenting the phenomenon in *Resurrecting Jesus*, 269–99.

be understood as experiences of this type and that they are best explained as a kind of projection from the minds of the perceivers.

Some defenders of the resurrection have responded by emphasizing differences between apparitions of the dead and the accounts we have of the resurrection appearances.[8] The most significant difference in my judgment is that people who experience such apparitions do not tend to think that the deceased person has been raised from the dead. They think of what happened as an encounter with someone who has gone to another realm, but is somehow able to appear in this one. So, why did the disciples describe their experiences differently? It is possible that there was something about these appearances that led the disciples to speak of resurrection. But there may be other explanations. Perhaps hearing stories of the empty tomb combined with appearances of Jesus suggested a resurrection. Perhaps their Jewish background or the teaching of Jesus played a role. At any rate, the fact that they interpret their experiences differently from the way apparitions of the dead are typically interpreted is not enough to conclude with confidence that we are not dealing with a similar kind of experience.

To be clear, I am not claiming that the resurrection appearances were visionary experiences or that we should think of them as standard cases of apparitions of the dead, just that on the basis of the testimony available, we can't rule out the possibility that the appearances of Jesus involved something different from ordinary physical sensation. Acknowledging as much means acknowledging that someone who rejects the cognitive value of experiences that do not involve ordinary sensation has a viable way of rejecting the testimony that Jesus has been raised. But such an assessment is not the only possibility. Even if some or all of the appearances were visionary, they might still be taken to support claims the disciples made about the resurrection.

Some people will, of course, reject the idea that visionary experiences can tell us about objective reality. But someone who thinks, as I do, that reality has a spiritual dimension that our scientific theorizing does not capture may be more open to the possibility that some visions can be revelatory. People who have experiences that seem to go beyond ordinary sensation such as near-death experiences or mystical experiences or apparitions of someone who has died are often utterly convinced that they have encountered something real. Their conviction does not establish that they are correct, but unless we adopt worldview assumptions that rule out the possibility, their testimony sometimes seems worthy of being taken seriously.

---

8. Habermas, "Dale Allison's Resurrection," 303–13.

In the case of biblical reports of resurrection appearances, considerations that might lead us to think that they might be revelatory include the fact that the reports describe multiple appearances to different people. It is easier to think that something merely subjective is happening if we are dealing with one or only a few experiences, but harder as the reports become more numerous. The subjective interpretation is also challenged by instances in which multiple witnesses report experiencing the same event. Even if we accept the possibility of some kind of shared vision, it is far from obvious that a subjective interpretation is superior to thinking of what is experienced as a revelatory event.

Some Christians think that they can assemble the kind of evidence for the resurrection that should compel the assent of anyone who is rational. However, I think that what we decide about the resurrection depends not only on how rational we are and how good we are at tracing logical implications. It also depends on whether the kinds of assumptions and inclinations that shape our response to this claim leave room for the possibility that such an event actually occurred. People who presume a worldview that excludes the possibility of anyone rising from the dead are likely to think that virtually any alternative that cannot be ruled out as impossible is superior to accepting the claim that Jesus was raised.

In addition to differences arising from fundamental assumptions about the nature of things or about how we gain knowledge, we should also recognize that our assessment of the resurrection is related to our assessment of Jesus. The disciples who reported that Jesus had appeared to them started from a previous experience of Jesus and a faith in the God of Israel. What they knew of Jesus convinced them that he had extraordinary wisdom and power that were connected to a remarkable closeness to God. This response did not mean that they expected a resurrection. They did not. But when they had experiences of the risen Jesus, the question of his rising from the dead was not for them the general issue of whether some person can rise from the dead. It was instead the more specific question of whether this person, who had given every indication of having an incredibly close connection with the Creator of all, had been raised.

We cannot have their experiences, so in our case the assessment we make of Jesus depends on whether we find the stories that early Christians told about Jesus impressive enough to entertain the idea that he could reveal God in a unique way. If not, we are unlikely to be convinced by whatever evidence we are given of the resurrection. Of course, our willingness to entertain such an idea presupposes accepting God's existence and understanding God to be the kind of being who can do things in the world. If you don't think God exists or you don't think God acts in the world, you will likely dismiss claims about the resurrection as too implausible to consider. Any alternative explanation of the events, even if it seems far-fetched in the extreme, is likely to be more acceptable to you.

Another relevant factor in our assessment of what happened is that the question of whether Jesus rose from the dead is not usually isolated from our response to the whole range of Christian teachings. People don't generally accept the resurrection and then decide separately what they think of Christianity as a whole. They typically view claims about the resurrection as part of a larger Christian account of things. I have argued in a different place that judgments about comprehensive accounts, such as the Christian one, should be understood in a practical context.[9] We need what I have called a *life-orienting story* to shape our understanding about how to live. So, for someone deciding about the resurrection, an important consideration is what kind of life-orienting story is to be put in the place of a Christian account, if the resurrection is rejected. Some people accept the resurrection because they find the larger story containing this event more compelling than any other story that might serve to guide their lives.

Coming to accept the Christian story is sometimes thought of in terms of giving assent to a number of factual claims. In one sense that description is correct. However, it is potentially misleading. Sometimes assenting to a fact makes sense only when you have undergone a significant shift in perspective. Or, to put it in another way, sometimes accepting a fact means accepting a whole new way to understand many other things. Evidence may play a role in shifts of this kind, but evidence is not the whole story. The kind of shift that leads one to think Jesus rose from the dead typically feels less like following a train of logical argument to a conclusion and more like what the Bible describes as having your eyes opened to something that was previously hidden.

This idea is illustrated dramatically in one of Luke's stories of a resurrection appearance. I do not know whether the story of the two people on the Emmaus Road told in Luke 24 is a historical event or not, but it portrays something profound about how revelatory experiences depend on what we are ready to receive. Two followers of Jesus are joined on the road by the risen Jesus, but they do not recognize him. It is only after they arrive at their destination when he blesses and breaks bread and gives it to them that the blinders are taken off and they realize who he is. No doubt this story says something about how Jesus was experienced in the early Christian community. But I think it is legitimate to extend it to say that responding to evidences of the resurrection involves more than just objectively considering

---

9. Holley, *Meaning and Mystery*, 11–30.

what can be demonstrated on the basis of established facts. The two in the story are described as "slow of heart." Recognizing the resurrection, we might say, involves opening our hearts in a way that enables us to expand our awareness.

Of course, that description is how it seems to someone who has accepted the resurrection. To someone who has not, biblical accounts may just seem incredible. Christians can acknowledge that these stories claim something that goes against the grain of our ordinary understanding of how the world works. In a way that is just the point. They portray an event that signals the advent of a new order that God is bringing about to replace the old familiar one. You can say that this kind of event does not fit in the world you know, but the issue is whether you are able to recognize in this event signs that point toward a transformation of this world.

Being able to consider such a possibility depends to a large extent on what you think of Jesus. The Emmaus Road disciples had been thinking that he was the one to restore Israel. For us, the question will be whether he is the one through whom God is restoring the world. Having such a hope does not automatically mean accepting the resurrection. But it does make it more likely that you can see the resurrection as something fitting and, hence, be open to signs that suggest it has actually happened.

For us, the main signs consist of testimony of early Christians who claimed to have encountered the risen Jesus. While this testimony does not compel the assent of everyone who is reasonable, it is enough to produce an inclination to believe in people who are in a receptive position. Those who have such an inclination can view their own inclination skeptically and veto it, or they can allow themselves to believe.[10] For those who can't decide one way or the other, but still find the Christian story more compelling than any alternative that might shape their lives, there is another option. It is to presume the truth of something you cannot verify and attempt to live on the basis of what you have presumed to be true. Sometimes this kind of response leads over time to belief, but even when it does not, it is one of the forms of what Christians have called faith.

---

10. Holley, "Practical Considerations and Evidence," 21–39.

Chapter 17

Learning to Love

ONE KIND OF TEST of whether you are a Christian is whether you accept the characteristic doctrines of Christianity as true. But while it is appropriate to think that there are beliefs involved in being a Christian, a different kind of test is prominent in some New Testament passages, a behavioral test. In its most general form, the test is whether you are living a life characterized by love for other people. Here is the way the test is explained in First John: "Beloved, let us love one another, because love is from God; everyone who loves is born of God and knows God. Whoever does not love does not know God, for God is love" (1 John 4:7–8). In other words, our treatment of others is a sign of whether or not we have made genuine contact with God. If we love others, we are living in harmony with God's nature. But if we don't love others, our claims to know God or to love God are revealed to be hollow (1 John 4:8, 20). Other New Testament passages portray a similar test. In the memorable judgment scene of Matt 25 the crucial question is whether we have shown compassion to those who are most vulnerable.

Some Christians are uncomfortable with the idea of a behavioral test because it sounds to them as if salvation is gained through performing good works. However, saying that loving acts are a sign of salvation does not imply that salvation is a reward for good behavior. We can affirm that salvation is a gift that we do not earn, while also affirming that the way we live reveals whether God's grace toward us is achieving its intended purposes. Immediately after the declaration in Ephesians that salvation comes about by grace through faith (Eph 2:8–9), we are told that we are "created in Christ Jesus for good works, which God prepared beforehand to be our way of life" (Eph 2:10).

I suspect that the discomfort some feel about a behavioral test of whether you are a Christian is closely connected with the thought that God might be sending people to heaven or hell based on whether their behavior is good enough. I agree that this picture of things gives us a distorted version of the Christian message, and I will say something relevant to correcting the distortion later in this chapter. However, it is also a distortion to think that the behavioral expectations described in the New Testament are irrelevant to whether you are a Christian. It is difficult to think that you could be a Christian without being a follower of Jesus, yet surely the answer to the question of whether you are following Jesus depends on how you are living, or at least how you are attempting to live.

To those who would be his disciples, Jesus gave instructions about how to live. But learning the way of life he taught involves a process that takes time. Think of the process as a kind of school in which you unlearn some habits and learn new ones.[1] Some of our habits of thinking, feeling and behaving block our ability to enter into the kind of love that Jesus invites us to embrace. Letting go of them and replacing them with different habits would free us to live a fuller kind of life, one that is in harmony with the urgings of God's Spirit, but some of what we would have to let go of is deeply ingrained. We take attitudes toward others that seem to us natural and unavoidable, but are in tension with fully recognizing their worth. We have attachments, such as concerns for personal security or status, that compete with concerns for the well-being of those around us. Learning new attitudes and redirecting our attachments does not come easily.

The difficulty is conveyed by the gospel saying that you have to lose your life in order to save it (Matt 16:25). Embracing this new way of life means letting go of what you may think you can't do without. To do so can feel like a major sacrifice. At the same time, the gospel message also speaks of a freedom and even an ease that comes with being able to let go of what is keeping you from a better kind of life. The ease, however, comes only after you have begun to put into practice what Jesus taught and as a result, internalized patterns of thinking and feeling that are conducive to consistently living this way. Following the path of discipleship instills habits that enable people to do what would have been difficult or even impossible previously. But additionally, the way of Christ can become easier in relation to alternative ways. Those who are well advanced in the path of discipleship acquire a perspective from which alternative ways of living come to seem less appealing, perhaps even unthinkable.

---

1. Norman Wirzba describes Christianity as a "training ground in the ways of love." See *Way of Love*, 4.

Ideally, the church facilitates the process of learning to follow Jesus. Discipleship was never intended to be a purely individual activity, but something we do with communal guidance, encouragement, and support. Unfortunately, for a variety of reasons, churches have often been poor at providing direction about how to live as Jesus instructed, sometimes not even realizing that this task was included in the command to make disciples, and sometimes promoting agendas that lead to a kind of self-righteousness and disparagement of others that is at odds with the kind of life followers of Jesus are called to live. So, there is a need for the Christian community to reflect seriously about what is involved in learning the way of living that Jesus taught.

JUDGING AND FORGIVENESS

Taken together, the teachings of Jesus can be understood as outlining a program for helping us dismantle barriers to the way of love. For example, one of the things that blocks our ability to love others is that we are so good at finding fault in them. The human tendency is to notice and condemn the faults of others, but to be less aware of, or even oblivious to, our own failings. We don't typically think that our judgments of our own behavior are biased. However, we find it easy to come up with rationalizations to justify what we do, and we reflexively take a defensive stance when others question it. One social scientist, citing research studies that show people who do bad things typically think that they are good people who are motivated by good reasons, suggests that we all have what he calls an "inner lawyer" whose job is to represent our own actions in the most favorable way. Further, we actually believe the stories our inner lawyer invents for these purposes.[2]

In response to our built-in tendencies to judge others more harshly than we judge ourselves, Jesus tells his followers not to judge, or perhaps not to judge unless they are willing to have the same kind of judgment applied in their own case. Using a memorable and picturesque image, he asks, "Why do you see the speck in your neighbor's eye, but do not notice the log in your own eye?" (Matt 7:3). If we had a more realistic understanding of our own faults, we might not be so quick to call attention to the faults of others. But we are prone to adopt a point of view that hides our own flaws, while highlighting other people's failings.

Of course, Jesus knew as well as anyone that never finding fault with another person is not a realistic option. Some negative judgments are proper and even inevitable. Jesus makes negative judgments himself when he

2. Haidt, *Happiness Hypothesis*, 63–64.

calls the religious leaders of his time hypocrites, and we can't have a sense of justice without being able to recognize some instances of injustice. The problem for most of us, however, is that our fault-finding gives expression to a presumption of superiority that gets in the way of more loving responses. When we set ourselves up to pronounce someone guilty, we don't usually do it out of concern for the other person's well-being. Often, it is a way of putting the other person down a peg or claiming the moral high ground for ourselves, and the attitudes toward others that accompany our pronouncements tend to crowd out more charitable thoughts about them. So, following the way of love means that our tendency toward fault-finding needs to be tempered. Instead of allowing it free rein, we need to cultivate the habit of restraining the urge to call attention to the failings of others.

It is not hard to see that restraint of this sort is often wise. We can recognize that the judgments we are inclined to make are often presumptuous. How often do we reach a judgment in anger without attending to relevant facts or in ignorance of considerations that would lead us to revise our judgments? How often are we rigid and unsympathetic in the way we apply our standards? How often are we using our judgments to hurt the other person?

What Jesus says about not seeing the log in our own eyes suggests a rule of thumb that we might use to restrain our tendency to make pronouncements about the faults of others. Suppose we consider their failings from the same kind of perspective we apply to our own behavior. If we would make excuses in our own case, shouldn't we be ready to consider the same kinds of excuses from others? More generally, if we would give ourselves the benefit of the doubt, shouldn't we be ready to do the same with others? Most of us are skilled at finding ways to avoid admitting fault in our own case. So, perhaps we should apply these skills to considering how the faults that we are so eager to point out may be less clear-cut than they might initially seem or to considering whether there are reasons for adjusting our assumptions of how blameworthy someone is. With some effort, we may be able to apply to assessments of others the same kinds of charitable interpretations that come so easily when we consider our own acts.

But what if the fault is genuine? What if we have exercised restraint, but the judgment of wrongdoing is unavoidable? Can we then make a judgment? Often, we can, but there is another teaching of Jesus that may apply in such a situation. We should be ready to forgive. Forgiving actually presupposes that we have made a judgment that someone has done wrong. Otherwise, there is no need to forgive. But Jesus's teachings about forgiveness tell us what to do when we make such a judgment. His teaching is difficult to put into practice, and it goes against strong inclinations. It often violates our common sense, and sometimes it seems absolutely crazy, or at least utterly misguided. But the instruction is not unclear. Jesus teaches that when others have wronged us, we should forgive them. I understand the forgiveness he calls for to mean refusing to hold the wrong against the other person and relinquishing our desires to hurt that person.

But why? We all have a strong sense that people should be held accountable for what they do, and forgiving can often feel like not standing up for yourself or for someone you care about. However, we should not confuse forgiveness with papering over a misdeed or pretending that there was no real wrong done, and a willingness to forgive does not exclude efforts to protect yourself and others from continued victimization. In the most admirable cases of forgiveness the refusal to seek retribution is not a matter of lacking self-respect. Instead, it proceeds from an unwillingness to enter into the kind of cycles of ill will that so often poison human relationships. At its best, forgiveness is a display of love that results in a willingness to give to others more than they deserve, and often it is a recognition that bad behavior is bound up with the kind of ignorance and confusion that pervade the human condition.

People in our day sometimes suggest that forgiving others should be done for our own peace of mind, that an unforgiving spirit leads to internal bitterness that in the end hurts us. While the suggestion is not without merit, it is not really the focus of the instruction of Jesus. Christian forgiveness is rooted in the thought that even those who have done terrible things have a potential for reformation that may be triggered by the experience of grace. By holding firmly to a vision of what the other person might be, we can lay down our obsession with the need to exact retribution and replace it with a concern for redemption of someone who has strayed from the path. A fuller awareness of our own failings can help us see the need to extend grace to others. Jesus portrays forgiveness of others as flowing from a realization that God forgives us. In his model prayer we ask for forgiveness as we affirm that we also forgive those who have wronged us.

I do not understand this teaching about forgiveness to tell us how a judicial system should operate. Societies need to enforce their laws if the laws are to achieve their social purposes. But in our individual relations, setting ourselves up to bring retribution on others is a recipe for continued conflict, and harboring ill will against one who has done us wrong often undercuts the possibility of a more fruitful relationship. To be sure, forgiveness may be abused by the offender; the practice of forgiveness means taking a risk. But sometimes forgiving leads to a response of gratitude and to a willingness to move beyond hostile attitudes. We have all heard stories of relationships that were broken until someone took the initiative to forgive.

Nevertheless, to forgive someone of a wrong is difficult, partly because it means absorbing pain yourself instead of seeking to inflict pain on another. This kind of suffering is at the heart of the Christian message. The deep truth here is that genuinely loving others means accepting the kind of suffering that goes with caring enough to seek their good even when it costs you.

The pain that goes with forgiveness can be overwhelming. When the wrong done is a major one, forgiveness may seem out of the question. However, we should recall that the Gospel of Luke describes Jesus forgiving those who crucified him, and some Christians throughout the centuries have followed his example in cases of extreme wrongs. For most of us, forgiveness of a major wrong is not something we can do immediately. Even if we want to forgive or think that we should forgive, it may take time to get to the point where we are able to do so. Jesus's instruction to pray for our enemies may help to get us to that point. But regardless of the difficulty, we can regard obedience to the teaching of Jesus to forgive to be the only acceptable alternative and work to reach the point where we are able to respond in love instead of hostility.

ANGER AND NONRETALIATION

The difficulty of forgiving is closely connected with the difficulty of laying down our anger. Anger is often an automatic response when we perceive that someone has wronged us. It is a response that is built into the programming of our bodily systems. We can recognize that anger serves a useful purpose in human relations. It functions as a signal to those who abuse others of the need to back off. It alerts people to protect themselves or protect others from someone who has violated the rules of proper behavior.

However, anger also has a downside. Jesus focuses on the connection between anger and violence. He traces acts of murder to getting into the kind of angry state conducive to thoughts and intentions to harm or to kill another person (Matt 5:21–26). He is obviously not saying that anger always has this result, but he is saying that being filled with rage toward someone, puts us on dangerous ground. Not only can things escalate beyond control. The response of anger tends to fuel our tendency toward self-righteousness and to hide from our view less hostile ways of responding to others.

When we are angry, we are making the kind of judgment of others that Jesus warns us about. Anger is not just a feeling, but expresses a construal that someone has done wrong. Our bodily states reinforce our construal and predispose us to defend ourselves against the wrongdoer in verbal and nonverbal ways. The judgments that we make in the angry state are typically not nuanced ones that take into account all the relevant considerations. While they are sometimes correct, they often involve overly simplified ways of thinking about what has happened. So, if we take Jesus to be warning us about finding fault generally, we might understand his teaching about anger as warning that we need to question our angry responses and to learn to restrain them.

One strategy of restraint is to develop the practice of refraining from some kinds of behaviors that an angry state might provoke. Jesus's teaching not to retaliate for wrongs done to us exemplifies this kind of restraint. Following a policy of not retaliating guards against the danger of anger escalating beyond control. But there is a broader reason for the practice of nonretaliation. Retaliation against others conflicts with forgiving them. If you think that forgiveness is the proper Christian response, then you should recognize that reserving the right to retaliate for wrongs done is antithetical to the Christian way of life. Paul echoes the teaching of Jesus when he says that vengeance should be left to God (Rom 12:19). But Paul goes a step further. He teaches that the Christian response to those who do wrong to you is to do good to them (Rom 12:20–21). What he says is in harmony with the teaching of Jesus to love even to those we would classify as enemies.

The instruction to do good to those who harm us goes against strong intuitions that are both biologically and culturally based. Our intuitions are structured by the principle of reciprocity: Do good to those who do good to you, but take a hostile stance toward those who mistreat you. Sometimes this standard is called the copper rule: Treat others as they treat you. This rule describes how people generally behave. But it contrasts significantly with the golden rule that Jesus endorses. Treating others as you want to be treated calls for doing good to others even when you do not expect to receive good treatment in return. When people live in accordance with the golden rule, their behavior can be surprising, even startling, for people who have been socialized to think in terms of the principle of reciprocity.

Nonretaliation and forgiveness can seem utterly naïve. They can seem like ways of losing at the game of life and allowing others to take advantage of us. But Jesus seems to be questioning our competitive orientation. He would not be persuaded by the claim that pursuing our own personal advantage is just what people do. Instead of thinking about how human life is generally lived, he focuses on what God intends it to be. He conceives of the life God intends not as an unrelenting struggle for wealth or power or status, but as participation in a community in which people care for each other, especially those who are most vulnerable. In the kingdom community, people are willing to give up personal advantage when doing so is needed for the good of the others. The commitment to follow Jesus is a commitment to behave in this way.

IS JESUS TOO IDEALISTIC?

The vision of such a community is likely to strike many people as idealistic in the extreme. However, we should notice three things. First, what is envisioned is rooted in a changed kind of motivation, but this motivation is not alien to human nature. It is to a large extent an expansion of capacities for empathy and compassion that are natural to us, but have been suppressed or not encouraged by social orders that have predisposed us toward greed and violence. Second, the way of living Jesus calls for is not to be achieved through individual effort alone, but with the help of a community that shapes people to live as God intends instead living by the values of earthly systems that have deceived and misshaped us. Third, the new way of life is made possible by a divine initiative that is the culmination of the prophetic expectation of Hebrew Scriptures that God's presence would have a transforming influence. In this vision, the human potential to behave in better ways is empowered by the divine Spirit.

Consider motivation first. The human motivational structure is complex. It is often oversimplified, as when it is claimed that all human behavior is motivated by self-interest. Some have thought that any action done for the benefit of another needs to be explained in self-interested terms. But unless we distort the evidence, we can recognize that humans sometimes have desires to alleviate the suffering of others that do not arise from any desire for personal gain. These desires are connected with our capacity for empathetic reactions. Sometimes empathy is described as the ability to put yourself in the other person's shoes. However, empathetic reactions involve something more than imaginative thinking; they involve actually feeling what others are experiencing. Our capacity to do so varies. Psychopaths are sometimes described as lacking ordinary human capacities for empathy, and in those who have what we think of as normal capacities, the compassion that comes from empathy may be suppressed by cultural shaping or by competing desires or emotions. Even so, feeling the kind of compassion that leads to acting for the good of others is part of the normal human motivational repertoire. Moreover, it is possible to cultivate this motivation so that it plays a larger role in shaping behavior. In other words, people can learn to be more empathetic and compassionate.

In the Gospels Jesus is frequently described as being moved by compassion when he encounters those in need. His compassion is triggered when he sees people as "like sheep without a shepherd" (Matt 9:36) and by his awareness of suffering to which he responds with healing acts. We might think of this sort of compassion as arising naturally when we become aware of other's needs, but failing to arise when our attention is focused elsewhere. Some teachings of Jesus can be understood as telling us to redirect our attention from concerns that can interfere with compassionate responses to those in need, such as the desire for wealth. Jesus warns that receptivity to his message can be choked off by "cares of the world and the lure of wealth" (Matt 13:22). The parable of the rich man and Lazarus (Luke 16:19–30) portrays a wealthy man whose addiction to extravagance has made him insensitive to the urgent need of others.

However, Jesus calls for an expansion of compassionate responses beyond what we usually think of as normal. While we are "wired" for compassion toward those in our group, our biological and cultural heritage inclines us to respond differently to outsiders. But Jesus rejects the divisions we make between people whose needs should concern us and those that we can treat as outside our sphere of concern. His well-known parable of the Good Samaritan portrays the ethnic and religious alien who is "moved with pity" toward a fellow human being from a group that despises people like him as someone to imitate (Luke 10:25–37).

While it is easy to affirm that the kind of expansive love demonstrated by the Good Samaritan is admirable, we should recognize that it involves a willingness to prioritize the needs of others in a way that may call for personal sacrifice. Consistently living in this way is unlikely to happen without a community that affirms our common humanity and teaches us that concern for others is vitally important. However, it is not enough just to be taught this kind of ideal; you have to learn to practice it. Norman Wirzba suggests this kind of learning requires a community in which love is modeled and supported: "To learn to love, you have to practice with other people who are committed to inspire you when you are tired, celebrate when you succeed, and comfort you when you fail."[3] Obviously, Christian churches have often failed be this kind of community. But the core teachings of the Christian community have sometimes prepared people to extend love to the stranger who needs help.

During research into the nature of evil, Philip Hallie came across an example of what he described as goodness that had been displayed by the people of a small village in France during Nazi occupation.[4] Defying the governing powers who had ordered Jews be rounded up and sent to

---

3. Wirzba, *Way of Love*, 21.
4. Hallie, *Lest Innocent Blood*.

concentration camps, this community, at significant risk, opened its doors to Jewish refugees, mostly children, helping large numbers escape across the mountains to Switzerland. Years after the war, Hallie visited this village and interviewed many of the people who had participated in the rescue effort. He recognized that their action was rooted in their Christian faith. Under the leadership of a remarkable pastor, they had absorbed the biblical injunction to protect the innocent. They had learned to see oppressed peoples as neighbors who needed their help. When Hallie told them that what they had done was heroic, they seemed uncomprehending. They responded that these people came to their doors. What else could they do? They had been formed by their religious heritage in such a way that aiding the victims of oppression wasn't seen as a choice at all. It was simply what must be done.

The Christian community has often been less successful in extending the motivation to aid the oppressed to efforts to reform societal systems. Christians have many times failed to see the victims of economic structures that work to the advantage of those who are well off, but exploit the poor and vulnerable. They have too often taken for granted social hierarchies that lead to abuse of power. Nevertheless, if we take a long historical view, the Christian message has been undeniably effective in focusing attention on the victim in a way that was historically unprecedented, leading to numerous movements to change unjust practices or to establish social institutions, such as orphanages and hospitals, to serve those in need. David Bentley Hart in describing how Christianity shifted ways of thinking that were taken for granted in the ancient world speaks of how ancients perceived a "bizarre prodigality with which Christians were willing to grant full humanity to persons of every class and condition, and of either sex."[5] Contemporary secular thinkers often fail to realize the extent to which their conception of social justice is rooted in this Christian moral vision.

A fuller answer to the question of whether the hope of a new community is too idealistic depends on whether we can conceive such a community as instrumental to God's action in the world. Hebrew prophets looked forward to a time when God's Spirit would be poured out in an unprecedented way, and early Christians believed that Jesus's life, death, and resurrection had made possible a new kind of connection with God's Spirit. A prominent New Testament claim is that God's presence, which had previously been associated with the Jewish temple, could now be experienced corporately and individually in the Christian community. Paul tells Christians, " . . . you are God's temple and God's Spirit dwells in you" (1 Cor 3:16). God's Spirit is understood to provide a kind of energy that pulls followers of Jesus toward

---

5. Hart, *Atheist Delusions*, 169.

loving relationships with others. Paul speaks of what he calls the "fruit of the Spirit" (Gal 5:22–26) that comes about when we allow ourselves to be "guided by the Spirit" (Gal 5:25). So, the vision is that the new community becomes possible as people align themselves with a transformative power that comes from God.

In chapter 12 I claimed that we should reject the idea that God has total control over everything that happens or that God can do whatever we imagine possible. Instead, I suggested that what God can do in the world depends on the cooperation of finite beings. We can think of that cooperation as activating channels through which God can influence what happens. I think that in Jesus an unprecedented submission to God opened channels through which God could do remarkable things and that as the followers of Jesus identified with him, they experienced a connection with God's Spirit that allowed God to act through them. Signs and wonders are part of it, but the presence of God is shown more generally in guiding people about what to do and in empowering them to achieve difficult things.

Given this understanding, a fundamental task of the Christian community is to shape people to be receptive to the presence and power of God. Thinking in these terms shows the importance of teaching disciplines such as prayer and meditation. One way that prayer can help is by decentering us from our self-focus. As finite beings in a physical world, we habitually view reality in terms of what promotes or constricts our individual aims. But prayer at its best involves a shift to a wider point of view. Even when we start with thoughts about our personal desires and needs, taking these concerns to God can be a means of learning to think about what we want from the perspective of what God is seeking to do. Mature prayer is not a matter of trying to get God to satisfy our wants, but of aligning our wants with God's purposes. Efforts to do so can create conditions under which God's Spirit can work through us.

One useful meditative exercise involves observing our own thoughts and reactions with a kind of dispassionate objectivity. Doing so can make us aware of the extent to which our default mode of operation is egocentric. We react to things in terms of how they affect us for good or ill, and we identify with the self that makes judgments from this perspective. But by detaching ourselves from this narrow point of view, we can sometimes discover how much it blocks us from seeing clearly. When we can recognize our self-serving rationalizations without endorsing them, we open the door to a realization that we are potentially more than this constricted kind of self.

Through the path of discipleship, we seek to transcend the limited focus of the ego-driven perspective by identifying with the Spirit of Christ.

Such an identification can be thought of as leading to an expanded awareness in which our neighbor evokes our compassion. Sometimes Christians describe this kind of shift as God's love flowing through them. It is not that our individual consciousness is replaced. It is rather that capacities we have as finite beings are enhanced. We move closer to becoming finite images of the divine source through which God's nature is expressed and our own nature is fulfilled.

THE CONSUMMATION

Many Christians think of the ultimate goal for human beings as going to heaven. Some New Testament passages do suggest an intermediate state after death, which has been called paradise, in which Christians who die are described as being with Christ, but such a state is not presented as the end goal. The focus of New Testament thought about the future is not just continued existence in some nonearthly realm, but the new creation or what N. T. Wright calls "life after life after death."[6] In the new creation heaven is united with earth, or we could say that heaven comes to earth. In this way of conceiving things, heaven is not so much a place, but the presence of God, and when this presence permeates earthly existence, the kind of human community God intends can become a reality.

I said near the beginning of this chapter that ideas about God sending people to heaven or hell based on whether their behavior measures up involve a distortion of the Christian message. The kind of distortion I have in mind arises primarily from thinking that our situation in the afterlife is best conceived in terms of some reward or punishment that is given to us, rather than thinking of it as a product of what we have become. We either learn the way of love, which allows us to participate in the joys of the resurrection community, or we hold onto things that keep us from the kind of human existence that God wants for us. If we ask questions such as whether some will be excluded from the consummation that the New Testament describes, perhaps the best answer is that resurrection life does exclude some things that have been a part of life in our world, and those who are unable or unwilling to give up what is inconsistent with a community built on love will not be able to participate in such a community. But what that amounts to largely speculative, despite the confident pronouncements that Christians sometimes make.

With regard to the new creation, there are suggestions in Scripture that point us in the direction of thinking that many of the things that have

6. Wright, *Surprised By Hope*, 151.

brought misery in earthly life, such as disease and death and armed conflict, are relegated to the past. There are also hints of new powers for human beings that are connected with a harmonious relationship to the earthly environment. We should probably also imagine that the fuller presence of God might free us from destructive tendencies that have plagued us and enable us to fulfill aspects of our nature that have been undeveloped.

Some people imagine that it will be a state of complete perfection. However, I don't think we need to conceive of the resurrection community as a state in which all human flaws magically disappear, though we might think that the incentives are weighted more in the direction of loving and creative ways of being instead of the destructive ones we have been accustomed to. I imagine it as a state in which there are tasks to be done and in which it is possible to perform those tasks with varying degrees of success or failure. I also imagine it as involving the opportunity for continued growth and continued learning. But in whatever way we try to fill in the details, the resurrection community should be thought of as a fulfillment of the divine project of creating finite beings who are able to be channels through which the infinite Love that is the source of all things can be expressed.

Bibliography

Allison, Dale. *Resurrecting Jesus: The Earliest Christian Tradition and Its Interpreters*. New York: T. and T. Clark, 2005.
Auden, W. H. "Introduction." In *The Protestant Mystics*, edited by Anne Freemantle, 13–38. New York: New American Library, 1964.
Augustine. *Expositions on the Book of Psalms*. In *Nicene and Post-Nicene Fathers*, first series, 8. Edited by Philip Schaff. Peabody, MA: Hendrickson, 1994.
———. *The Literal Meaning of Genesis*, vol. 1. In *Ancient Christian Writers* 41. Translated and annotated by John Hammond Taylor, SJ. New York: Paulist, 1982.
Austen, Jane, *Emma*. Boston: Houghton Mifflin, 1957.
Bailey, Kenneth. *Jesus Through Middle Eastern Eyes: Cultural Studies in the Gospels*. Downers Grove, IL: InterVarsity, 2008.
Berger, Peter. *Questions of Faith: A Skeptical Affirmation of Christianity*. Malden, MA: Blackwell, 2004.
Boyd, Gregory. *Cross Vision: How the Crucifixion of Jesus Makes Sense of Old Testament Violence*. Minneapolis: Fortress, 2017.
———. *The Myth of a Christian Nation: How the Quest for Political Power is Destroying the Church*. Grand Rapids: Zondervan, 2005.
Braude, Stephen. *Crimes of Reason: On Mind, Nature, and the Paranormal*. Lanham, MD: Rowman and Littlefield, 2014.
———. *ESP and Psychokinesis: A Philosophical Analysis*. Rev. ed. Parkland, FL: Brown Walker, 2002.
Brownson, James V. *Bible, Gender, Sexuality: Reframing the Church's Debate on Same-Sex Relationships*. Grand Rapids: Eerdmans, 2013.
Carr, David M. *Reading the Fractures of Genesis: Historical and Literary Approaches*. Louisville: Westminster John Knox, 1996).
Clifford, Richard J. *Creation Accounts in the Ancient Near East and in the Bible*. Washington, DC: Catholic Biblical Association of America, 1994.
Dawkins, Richard. *The God Delusion*. Boston: Houghton Mifflin, 2006.
Enns, Peter. *The Bible Tells Me So: Why Defending Scripture Has Made Us Unable to Read It*. New York: Harper Collins, 2014.
———. *How the Bible Actually Works*. New York: HarperCollins, 2019.
———. *Inspiration and Incarnation*. 2nd ed. Grand Rapids: Baker, 2015.
Epictetus, *Enchiridion*. Translated by Thomas W. Higginson. New York: Liberal Arts, 1950.
Evans, C. Steven. *Philosophy of Religion*. Downers Grove, IL: InterVarsity, 1985.

Flood, Derek. *Healing the Gospel: A Radical Vision for Grace, Justice, and the Cross*. Eugene, OR: Cascade, 2012.

Grosso, Michael. *Smile of the Universe: Miracles in an Age of Disbelief*. San Antonio, TX: Anomalist, 2020.

Griffin, David Ray. *Parapsychology, Philosophy, and Spirituality: A Postmodern Exploration*. New York: State University of New York Press, 1997.

Habermas, Gary. "Dale Allison's Resurrection Skepticism: A Critique." *Philosophia Christi* 10 (2008) 303–13.

Haidt, Jonathan. *The Happiness Hypothesis: Finding Modern Truth in Ancient Wisdom*. New York: Basic, 2006.

Hallie, Philip. *Lest Innocent Blood Be Shed: The Story of the Village of Le Chambon and How Goodness Happened There*. New York: Harper Perennial, 1994.

Hart, David Bentley. *The Atheist Delusions: The Christian Revolution and Its Fashionable Enemies*. New Haven, CT: Yale University Press, 2009.

Hays, Richard. *The Moral Vision of the New Testament: A Contemporary Introduction to New Testament Ethics*. New York: HarperCollins, 1996.

Hick, John. *The Fifth Dimension: An Exploration of the Spiritual Realm*. Oxford: Oneworld, 1999.

Holley, David M. *Meaning and Mystery: What It Means to Believe in God*. Malden, MA: Wiley Blackwell, 2010.

———. "Practical Considerations and Evidence in James's Permission to Believe." *Religious Studies* 51 (2015) 21–39.

Hume, David. *An Inquiry Concerning Human Understanding*. Cambridge: Cambridge University Press, 2007.

James, William. *The Varieties of Religious Experience*. New York: New American Library, 1958.

Jersak, Bradley. *Her Gates Will Never Be Shut: Hope, Hell, and the New Jerusalem*. Eugene, OR: Wipf & Stock, 2009.

———. *A More Christlike God: A More Beautiful Gospel*. Pasadena, CA: CWR, 2015.

Justin. *Apology*. In *Early Christian Fathers*. Translated and edited by Cyril C. Richardson, 242–89. Philadelphia: Westminster, 1953.

Keener, Craig S. *Miracles: The Credibility of the New Testament Accounts*, vols. 1–2. Grand Rapids: Baker, 2011.

Kelly, Edward, et. al. *Beyond Physicalism: Towards Reconciliation of Science and Spirituality*. Lanham, MD: Rowman and Littlefield, 2015.

———. *Irreducible Mind: Toward a Psychology for the 21st Century*. Lanham, MD: Rowman and Littlefield, 2007.

Kraybill, Donald B. *The Upside-Down Kingdom*. Scottdale, PA: Harold, 1978.

Kraybill, Donald B., et al. *Amish Grace: How Forgiveness Transcended Tragedy*. Hoboken, NJ: Jossey-Bass, 2010.

Lewis, C. S. *The Great Divorce*. New York: Macmillan, 1946.

———. *The Problem of Pain*. New York: Macmillan, 1962.

Mendelsohn, I. "Slavery in the OT." In *Interpreter's Dictionary of the Bible*, 4:383–91. New York: Abingdon, 1962.

Merritt, Jonathan. *A Faith of Our Own: Following Jesus Beyond the Culture Wars*. New York: FaithWords, 2012.

Newbigin, Lesslie. *Proper Confidence: Faith, Doubt, and Certainty in Christian Discipleship*. Grand Rapids: Eerdmans, 1995.

Piper, John. "How Can Evil Ever Have a Good Purpose?" http://www.desiringgod.org/interviews/how-can-evil-have-a-good-purpose.
Polkinghorne, John. *The Faith of a Physicist: Reflections of a Bottom-Up Thinker.* Princeton: Princeton University Press, 1994.
———. "Kenotic Creation and Divine Action." In *The Work of Love: Creation as Kenosis*, edited by John Polkinghorne, 90–106. Grand Rapids: Eerdmans, 2001.
Radin, Dean. *The Conscious Universe: The Scientific Truth of Psychic Phenomena.* New York: HarperCollins, 1997.
———. *Supernormal: Science, Yoga, and the Evidence for Extraordinary Psychic Abilities.* New York: Crown, 2013.
Sanford, Agnes. *The Healing Gifts of the Spirit.* New York: J. B. Lippincott, 1966.
Schmicker, Michael. *Best Evidence.* 2nd ed. New York: Writers Club, 2002.
Scholem, Gershom G. *Major Trends in Jewish Mysticism.* New York: Schocken, 1961.
Sparks, Kenneth L. *God's Word in Human Words: An Evangelical Appropriation of Critical Biblical Scholarship.* Grand Rapids: Baker, 2008.
Stewart, Robert, ed. *The Resurrection of Jesus: John Dominic Crossan and N. T. Wright in Dialogue.* Minneapolis: Fortress, 2006.
Swinburne, Richard. *Faith and Reason.* 2nd ed. Oxford: Clarendon, 2005.
Tart, Charles T. *The End of Materialism: How Evidence of the Paranormal is Bringing Science and Spirit Together.* Oakland, CA: New Harbinger, 2009.
Taylor, Steve. *Spiritual Science: Why Science Needs Spirituality to Make Sense of the World.* London: Watkins Media, 2018.
Tertullian. *Apology.* In *Ante-Nicene Fathers*, edited by Philip Schaff, 3:17–60. Grand Rapids: Christian Classics Ethereal Library, 2006.
Tolstoy, Leo. *The Death of Ivan Ilyich and Confession.* Translated by Peter Carson. New York: Liveright, 2014.
Vines, Matthew. *God and the Gay Christian.* New York: Convergent, 2014.
Walton, John H. *Old Testament Theology.* Downers Grove, IL: InterVarsity, 2017.
Walton, John and Harvey Walton. *Demons and Spirits in Biblical Theology: Reading the Biblical Text in its Cultural and Literary Context.* Eugene, OR: Cascade, 2019.
Ward, Keith. *What the Bible Really Teaches: About Crucifixion, Resurrection, Salvation, the Second Coming, and Eternal Life.* New York: Crossroads, 2005.
White, Victor. *God and the Unconscious.* Chicago: Henry Regionary, 1953.
Willard, Dallas. *The Divine Conspiracy: Rediscovering Our Hidden Life in God.* San Francisco: Harper Collins, 1998.
Wink, Walter. *Engaging the Powers: Discernment and Resistance in a World of Domination.* Minneapolis: Fortress, 1992.
———. *The Powers That Be: Theology for a New Millennium.* New York: Doubleday, 1998.
Wirzba, Norman. *Way of Love: Recovering the Heart of Christianity.* New York: HarperCollins, 2016.
Wolterstorff, Nicholas. "Reading Joshua." In *Divine Evil?: The Moral Character of the God of Abraham*, edited by Michael Bergmann, et al., 236–56. Oxford: Oxford University Press, 2011.
Wright, N. T. *The Day the Revolution Began: Reconsidering the Meaning of Jesus's Crucifixion.* New York: HarperOne, 2016.
———. *Jesus and the Victory of God.* Minneapolis, Minnesota: Fortress, 1996.
———. *The Resurrection of the Son of God.* Minneapolis, Minnesota: Fortress, 2003.

———. *Surprised By Hope: Rethinking Heaven, the Resurrection, and the Mission of the Church.* New York: HarperCollins, 2008.

Yoder, John Howard. *The Politics of Jesus.* Grand Rapids: Eerdmans, 1972.

Zahnd, Brian. *A Farewell to Mars: An Evangelical Pastor's Journey Toward the Biblical Gospel of Peace.* Colorado Springs: David C. Cook, 2014.

Index

Allison, Dale, 162, 163
Augustine, 8, 39, 105, 151
Austen, Jane, 13
animal sacrifice, 62–64, 86
atonement, 81–89
    the cross as revelation, 87–89
    metaphors for Jesus's work, 86–87
    penal substitutionary theory, 82, 83, 85
Anselm, 81
altered states of consciousness, 122–24, 128
Auden, W. H., 123
Amish, 150, 153
anger, 7, 45, 46, 99, 140, 145, 150, 170, 172–74

behavioral test of being a Christian, 167–68
biblical interpretation, 31–78
    allegorical, 39
    anthropomorphism, 45–47
    control beliefs, 46
    creation stories, 10, 34, 36, 52–54
    disagreement between authors, 59–66
    death penalty, 68–69, 151
    ethical guidance, 67–78
    exodus story, 56–57
    genre, 53, 56
    historical accuracy, 49–58
    historical-critical study, 32
    oral tradition, 55, 161
    same-sex sexuality, 75–78
    slavery, 70–73
    women, 73–75
Boyd, Gregory, 44, 102, 103–4, 152
Brownson, James, 77, 78

certainty-uncertainty, 17–19, 48, 160
Calvin, John, 81
Calvinist, 110
charisms, 128
creation as withdrawal, 112, 113
Celsus, 151
Constantine, 151
counter-cultural communities, 152
Caesar, 135, 159
compassion, 51, 135, 136, 167, 174–78
consummation, 178–79

Dawkins, Richard, 102
discipleship, 23, 91, 96–97, 168, 169, 177

Epictetus, 26–27
evil, problem of, 105
extrasensory perception, 128
enemies, Jesus's teaching about, 48, 91, 104, 135, 136, 143–54, 172, 173
empathy, 174
Enns, Peter, 44, 51, 52, 54, 56, 65
the excluded, 133–42
expansive love, 175–76

faith
    and evidence, 12–16
    firmness and flexibility, 4–5
    as a guide to life, 22–24

faith *(continued)*
   protection of, 24–27
   loss of, 21–28
   and receptiveness, 15, 115
   recognizing the signs, 14–16
   reflection on, 18, 19–20
forgiveness
   God's, 81, 82, 85, 104, 106, 144
   human, 89, 93, 135, 136, 148, 149, 150, 152, 158, 169–72, 173

God's control, 108–18
God's delight, 106–7
God's judgment, 6, 51, 61, 92, 95, 96, 98–107, 134, 145, 149, 167
God's presence, 6, 13, 21, 22, 98, 106, 115, 158, 174, 176, 177, 178, 179
Good Samaritan, 141, 143, 175

habits, 106, 168
Hallie, Philip, 175–76
Hasker, William, 113, 114
Hays, Richard, 153
Hick, John, 129, 130
Hume, David, 125
hell, 5–6, 81, 92, 94, 96, 104–6, 168, 178
henotheism, 37

James, William, 122, 123, 124
Jersak, Bradley, 103, 104–5
Job, 9, 51, 60–62
Jonah, 9, 10, 50–51
Jubilee, 71, 139–41
judging others, 169–70

kenosis, 113
kingdom of God, 27, 133, 134–36, 142, 143, 152, 158

Lewis, C. S., 5–6, 105
liberation, 139, 140, 156, 158
life-orienting story, 165

Martyr, Justin, 151
Messiah, 20, 65, 66, 86, 134–35, 137, 139, 156–57, 159
meditation, 128, 129, 177

miracles, 114–16, 124–26, 130, 155–56
monotheism, 37
motivation, 15, 45, 83, 96, 174, 176
mystery, 13, 121
mystical experience, 123–24, 129, 163

new creation, 157–58, 159, 178
nonretaliation, 148, 172–74

open theists, 114

Patanjali, 128
placebo effect, 126–27
Piper, John, 110–11, 114
prodigal son, 9, 10, 82, 138
prayer, 27, 63, 92, 118–19, 127, 129, 145, 149, 171, 177
Polkinghorne, John, 112, 113, 116, 158
psychokinesis, 128
punishment, 51, 61, 67, 68, 71, 72, 81, 82, 83, 84, 94, 96, 98–107, 137, 141, 145, 146, 178
   organic, 103–4, 106
   judicial, 103–4

revelation, 10, 20, 31–40, 43, 44, 45, 47, 48, 51, 53, 58, 66, 69, 70, 78, 83, 84, 87–89, 96, 102, 104, 118, 155
   divine accommodation, 38, 39, 43
   human authors, 31–40
   progressive, 38, 39, 43, 44, 47, 78
resurrection of Jesus, 155–66
   appearances, 160–63
   belief in, 160–66
   biblical testimony, 160
   empty tomb, 161–62, 163
   New Testament understanding of, 156–59
righteousness and wickedness, 60–62

salvation, 90–97
   and community, 93
   as an event, 92–94
   as fulfillment, 6, 94–95, 179
   as going to heaven, 92, 93, 133

as a process, 92, 94–96
samyama, 128
scientific naturalism, 120, 121, 124, 126
secondary causes, 100, 101
Sheol, 34, 156
siddhis, 128
Sparks, Kenton, 38, 54, 72

Tolstoy, Leo, 21–22
Torah, 23, 65
Tertullian, 151

violence, 41–48, 143–54
   divine commands, 41–48
   early Christian tradition, 151–53
   Jesus's teaching about, 143–54
   just-war theory, 151–52
   myth of redemptive, 153
   pacifism, 151

Ward, Keith, 87, 115
wealth, 62, 140, 142, 173, 175
Willard, Dallas, 144
Wink, Walter, 34, 118, 146, 147–48, 153
Wirzba, Norman, 168, 175
Wright, N. T., 88, 89, 115, 133, 141, 158, 159, 178

Zahnd, Brian, 144

www.ingramcontent.com/pod-product-compliance
Lightning Source LLC
Chambersburg PA
CBHW031428150426
43191CB00006B/446